SHAKESPEARE QUARTOS
in collotype facsimile

No. 7

Hamlet
First Quarto, 1603

Hamlet

First Quarto, 1603

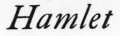

SHAKESPEARE QUARTO FACSIMILES
No. 7

With an introductory note by W. W. Greg

OXFORD
AT THE CLARENDON PRESS

In the Stationers' Register the following entry appears under the date 26 July 1602:

Iames   Entred for his Copie vnder the handes of m^r Pasfeild &
Robertes   m^r waterson warden A booke called the Revenge of
Hamlett Prince Denmarke as yt was latelie Acted by the
Lo: Chamberleyn his servantes   vj^d

[Register C, fol. 84 verso]

It was, we may suppose, rather in contravention than in pursuance of this entrance that the first edition appeared the following year. Roberts was in no way concerned in the publication, which has been traced to the press of Valentine Simmes, a disorderly printer who had repeatedly been in trouble and once for a while suppressed, and which bore the imprint 'for N.L. and Iohn Trundle', the initials being those of Nicholas Ling, whose device also appears on the title-page. Ling had been in regular business for a dozen years or more; Trundle had only taken up his freedom a few years earlier and was just embarking on his first ventures. Their association suggests that Trundle may have been responsible for procuring the copy, Ling for the financial side of the undertaking. The play is represented as having been 'acted by his Highnesse seruants', and the edition was therefore presumably issued after 19 May 1603 when the former Lord Chamberlain's men received their patent as servants of the King. It is a 'Bad Quarto', the text of which runs to no more than 2220 type-lines, whereas there are almost 3800 in the 'Good Quarto' of 1604–5.

Of this First Quarto only two copies are known, both imperfect: that discovered by Sir Henry Bunbury in 1823, formerly in the possession of the Duke of Devonshire and now in the Huntington Library, California, wants the last leaf; that in the British Museum, said to have been brought from Nottinghamshire to Dublin by a student of Trinity College, acquired by Halliwell in

1856, and sold to the Museum in 1858, wants the title-leaf; neither preserves the blank that probably once preceded the title. Apart from these defects both are in good condition, though in the Huntington copy a few headlines are shaved and those on the verso pages are obscured by the mounting paper, the leaves being inlaid; both have been to some extent defaced with annotations in pen and ink, more extensive in the Museum copy, but more serious in the Huntington, where at a number of points the reading of the text has been deliberately altered.

A lithographic facsimile was prepared in 1880* by W. Griggs under the direction of F. J. Furnivall from the Devonshire copy, and the same copy was reproduced in collotype by the Huntington Library in 1931. Both were supplemented from the Museum copy in respect of the last page. The present facsimile has been made from the Museum copy, except of course for the title-page, for which Huntington Library very kindly provided a photograph.†

For convenience of comparison the act and scene division of the standard text has been indicated in the margin of the present facsimile. But the great divergence of the texts as a rule precludes correspondence of detail. It is only here and there that the habitual method of line numbering by comparison with the Globe text is applicable: usually all that can be done is to indicate which

* An earlier facsimile of the First Quarto appears to have been issued by J. P. Collier in a few copies in 1858; a reprint was published as early as 1825.

† Three apparent variations between the Griggs facsmile and the present (D1, l.9, 'Ham.' for 'Mar.'; E1ᵛ, l. 7, 'backe,' for 'becke,'; F4ᵛ, l. 11, 'Ham.' for 'Hor.') are due to manuscript alterations having been incorporated in the facsimile; four (B1ᵛ, l.12, 'coarſe' for 'courſe'; H4, l. 34, 'ghoſt' for 'gheſt'; I2ᵛ, l.36, 'predeſtinate' for 'predeſtiuate'; I3, l.3, 'haue' for 'hane') are errors of the lithographer. Many of the headlines are faked.

lines of the received text offer some sort of parallel to those of the Quarto.* But though numbers have been freely inserted for this purpose, it should be emphasized that they are only intended to facilitate reference from one text to the other and make no pretence of affording a complete comparison between them. Thus although where substantial passages have been transferred from one scene to another the fact has been duly indicated, no attempt has been made to record the frequent borrowing of isolated lines or phrases.†

Reference to the text of the First Quarto is most

* It may be mentioned that a reference such as 135–7 means that the Quarto line opposite which it stands either contains the substance of lines 135 *to* 137 of the Globe text, or else contains elements at least of lines 135 *and* 137: a reference 137–5 means 137 *and* 135.

† These are for the most part recorded in the Furnivall facsimile. Thus D4^v, l. 23 (in II. ii) is marked as corresponding to III. i. 37 (which is perhaps doubtful); E2^v, ll. 25–6 (in II. ii) correspond to III. ii. 354–5; F1^v, l. 29 (in III. i) borrows from III. iii. 28; G2, l. 36 and G2^v, l. 1 (in III. iv) are parallel to I. v. 49–50; H2, ll, 27–8 (in IV. v) recall IV. vii. 25–6 (the next line is marked as coming from V. i. 27, which must be a mistake); H2^v, l. 1 (in IV. v) is marked as parallel to IV. vii. 29 (but the resemblance is remote); H2^v, l. 3 (in IV. v) is marked as parallel to IV. vii. 335 (but there is no such line: in fact ll. 3–4 distantly recall IV. vii. 33); in IV. vi (a scene not as a whole parallel with any in the standard text) H2^v, ll. 20 and 33 recall IV. vi. 24 and 28–9, and ll. 34 and 36 recall V. ii. 44–7 and 49–50. On the other hand some correspondences are overlooked. Corambis's line in II. ii (D4, l. 2), 'Now my Lord, touching the yong Prince Hamlet', is, of course, a recollection of Ophelia's line at I. iii. 89 ('So please you, something touching the Lord Hamlet'); Laertes's words in IV. vii (H3, l. 14), 'My will, not all the world', properly form IV. v. 137; and his exclamation later in the scene (H3^v, l. 7), 'O would the time were come!' rightly belongs to Hamlet at I. ii. 256 ('would the night were come!').

I have found Furnivall's numbering the greatest help in preparing that for the present facsimile, though frequent differences will be noticed. These are due to several causes: some divergence of system, some differences of opinion as to what is parallel and what is not, some miscounting of the Globe lines by Furnivall, and some definite errors.

conveniently made by signature and line, and to facilitate this a star has been placed in the margin opposite each tenth type-line of each page and a dot opposite each intervening fifth line (not counting the head and running titles). By observing these the number of each line can be ascertained at a glance.

A few readings are, for one reason or another, obscure in the facsimile. A comparison with the reproduction of the Huntington copy establishes the following readings:

B2ᵛ,	l. 3	For	D3,	l. 32	*Que.* (not colon)
B3,	l. 15	Lets	D4,	l. 4	effect,
	16	ſhall finde	E4,	l. 34	ore-teeming
B4ᵛ,	l. 33	*Capapea* (no			loynes,
		accent)	F1ᵛ,	l. 1	My lord,
C1ᵛ,	l. 29	riſe	F2,	l. 28	then
	33	ſay	G2,	l. 34	vertues are
D1ᵛ,	l. 6	i'ſt (*trace of apos-*	H1,	l. 15	mone,
		trophe)	H2,	l. 19	too't:
D2,	l. 7	ſweare. (*possible*	H2ᵛ,	l. 21	meete
		trace of period)	I4,	l. 17	kingdome,

The following are the pen-and-ink alterations observed in the facsimile of the Huntington copy:

B3,	l. 20	impudent [ud *altered to* ot]
	23	*Cornelia* [*a* altered to *o*]
D1,	l. 9	*Mar.* [crossed out and *Ham.* (or *Ham:*) written in the margin]
E1,	l. 25	bawd: [-ſooner, *added*]
E1ᵛ,	l. 5	It [As *prefixed and* I *apparently altered to* i]
	7	becke [*first* e *altered to* a]
E2,	l. 11	Gentlemen, [nt *apparently altered to* m (*presumably accidently*)]
F4,	l. 23	Epitithe, [*second* t *apparently altered to* p (*or possibly* it *to* ap)]
F4ᵛ,	l. 11	*Hor.* [*or.* altered to *am.*]

The following differences have been noted between the British Museum and Huntington copies:

B1ᵛ, l. 15   In BM there is a lead above and another below the
              direction: in Hunt. both leads are below it.
B3, l. 31   BM *Leartes*, . . . news : Hunt. *Leartes* . . . newes
      33   BM *Lea.* : Hunt. *Lea:*
B4, l. 7   BM God, . . . months . . . married: Hunt. God . . .
              moneths . . . maried
B4ᵛ, l. 14   BM father. : Hunt. father,
      35   BM eies : Hunt. eies.

In both formes of the sheet the British Museum copy
evidently exhibits the corrected state.

The clumsy mending of a small tear in the top of F4
of the Huntington copy is responsible, through a slight
overlap of the edges, for some *apparent* variants (the readings are actually the same in the two copies). These
apparent readings in the Huntington copy are:

F4, l. 1   inieſt,
      2   phy?
F4ᵛ, l. 1   Hepoyſons
      2   Liglts,
      3   Theking

Since reprints of the First Quarto have usually been
based on the Huntington copy they have as a rule
reproduced most of these pseudo-readings. An exception
is that in the original edition of the Cambridge Shake-
speare (1866, vol. viii, pp. 226-7) which has only the
first of them: the second edition (1893, vol. ix, pp.
729-30) has also the second, third, and fifth, probably
through reliance on the Griggs facsimile.

                                        W. W. G.

THE
Tragicall Historie of
HAMLET

Prince of Denmarke

By William Shake-speare.

As it hath beene diuerse times acted by his Highnesse seruants in the Cittie of London : as also in the two V-
niuersities of Cambridge and Oxford, and else-where

At London printed for N.L. and Iohn Trundell.
1603.

The Tragicall Historie of

HAMLET

Prince of Denmarke.

Enter two Centinels. { *now call'd Bernardo* & *Francisco* —

I.i.

1. STand: who is that?

2. STis I.

1-2

1. O you come most carefully vpon your watch,

5

2. And if you meete *Marcellus* and *Horatio*,

6

The partners of my watch, bid them make haste.

1. I will: See who goes there.

. 12

Enter Horatio and Marcellus.

Hor. Friends to this ground.

Mar. And leegemen to the Dane,

* 15

O farewell honest souldier, who hath releeued you?

1. *Barnardo* hath my place, giue you good night.

Mar. Holla, *Barnardo.*

2. Say, is *Horatio* there?

Hor. A peece of him.

2. Welcome *Horatio*, welcome good *Marcellus.*

20

Mar. What hath this thing appear'd againe to night.

2. I haue seene nothing.

Mar. *Horatio* sayes tis but our fantasie,

And wil not let beliefe take hold of him,

Touching this dreaded sight twice seene by vs,

25

B   There-

Therefore I haue intreated him a long with vs
To watch the minutes of this night,
That if againe this apparition come,
He may approoue our eyes, and speake to it.

   Hor. Tut, t'will not appeare.

30   2. Sit downe I pray, and let vs once againe
Assaile your eares that are so fortified,
What we haue two nights seene.

   Hor. Wel, sit we downe, and let vs heare *Bernardo* speake
of this.

35   2. Last night of al, when yonder starre that's west-
ward from the pole, had made his course to
Illumine that part of heauen. Where now it burnes,
The bell then towling one.

Enter Ghoſt.

40   *Mar.* Breake off your talke, see where it comes againe.

   2. In the same figure like the King that's dead,

   Mar. Thou art a scholler, speake to it *Horatio.*

   2. Lookes it not like the king?

   Hor. Most like, it horrors mee with feare and wonder.

   2. It would be spoke to.

45   *Mar.* Question it *Horatio.*

   Hor. What art thou that thus vsurps the state, in
Which the Maiestie of buried *Denmarke* did sometimes
Walke? By heauen I charge thee speake.

   Mar. It is offended.   *exit Ghoſt.*

50   2. See, it stalkes away.

   Hor. Stay, speake, speake, by heauen I charge thee
speake.

   Mar. Tis gone and makes no answer.

   2. How now *Horatio*, you tremble and looke pale,
Is not this something more than fantasie?

55 What thinke you on't?

   Hor. Afore my God, I might not this beleeue, without
the sensible and true auouch of my owne eyes.

Mar.

Mar. Is it not like the King?

Hor. As thou art to thy selfe,   60

Such was the very armor he had on,

When he the ambitious *Norway* combated.

So frownd he once, when in an angry parle   *Polack*

He smot the sleaded pollax on the yce,

Tis strange.

 Mar. Thus twice before, and iump at this dead hower,   65

With Marshall stalke he passed through our watch.

 Hor. In what particular to worke, I know not,   *

But in the thought and scope of my opinion,

This bodes some strange eruption to the state.

 Mar. Good, now sit downe, and tell me he that knowes   70

Why this same strikt and most obseruant watch,

So nightly toyles the subiect of the land,

And why such dayly cost of brazen Cannon

And forraine marte, for implements of warre,

Why such impresse of ship-writes, whose sore taske 75

Does not diuide the sunday from the weeke:

What might be toward that this sweaty march

Doth make the night ioynt labourer with the day,   *

Who is't that can informe me?

 Hor. Mary that can I, at least the whisper goes so,   80

Our late King, who as you know was by Forten-

Brasse of *Norway*,   82

Thereto prickt on by a most emulous cause, dared to

The combate, in which our valiant *Hamlet*,

For so this side of our knowne world esteemed him,   85

Did slay this Fortenbrasse,

Who by a seale compact well ratified, by law

And heraldrie, did forfeit with his life all those   *

His lands which he stoode seazed of by the conqueror,

Against the which a moity competent,

Was gaged by our King: 91

Now sir, yong Fortenbrasse,   95

Of inapproued mettle hot and full,

Hath in the skirts of *Norway* here and there,
Sharkevp a sight of lawlesse Resolutes
For food and diet to some enterprise,
That hath a stomacke in't : and this (I take it) is the
Chiefe head and ground of this our watch.

Enter the Ghost.

But loe, behold, see where it comes againe,
He crosse it, though it blast me : stay illusion,
If there be any good thing to be done,
That may doe ease to thee, and grace to mee,
Speake to mee.
If thou art priuy to thy countries fate,
Which happly foreknowing may preuent, O speake to me,
Or if thou hast extorted in thy life,
Or hoorded treasure in the wombe of earth,
For which they say you Spirites oft walke in death, speake
to me, stay and speake, speake, stoppe it *Marcellus*.

2. T is heere.   *exit Ghost.*

Hor. T is heere.

Marc. T is gone, O we doe it wrong, being so maiesti-
call, to offer it the shew of violence,
For it is as the ayre inuelmorable,
And our vaine blowes malitious mockery.

2. It was about to speake when the Cocke crew.

Hor. And then it faded like a guilty thing,
Vpon a fearefull summons : I haue heard
The Cocke, that is the trumpet to the morning,
Doth with his earely and shrill crowing throate,
Awake the god of day, and at his sound,
Whether in earth or ayre, in sea or fire,
The strauagant and erring spirite hies,
To his confines, and of the trueth heereof
This present obiect made probation.

Marc. It faded on the crowing of the Cocke,
Some say, that euer gainst that season comes,
Wherein our Sauiours birth is celebrated,

The

The bird of dawning singeth all night long,
And then they say, no spirite dare walke abroade,
The nights are wholesome, then no planet frikes, *strikes*
No Fairie takes, nor Witch hath powre to charme,
So gratious, and so hallowed is that time.

Hor. So haue I heard, and doe in parte beleeue it:
But see the Sunne in russet mantle clad,
Walkes ore the deaw of yon hie mountaine top,
Breake we our watch vp, and by my aduise,
Let vs impart what wee haue scene to night
Vnto yong *Hamlet*: for vpon my life
This Spirite dumbe to vs will speake to him:
Do you consent, wee shall acquaint him with it,
As needefull in our loue, fitting our duetie?

Marc. Lets doo't I pray, and I this morning know,
Where we shall finde him most conueniently.

Enter King, Queene, Hamlet, Leartes, Corambis,
and the two Ambassadors, with Attendants.

King Lordes, we here haue writ to *Fortenbrasse*,
Nephew to olde *Norway*, who impudent
And bed-rid, scarcely heares of this his
Nephews purpose : and Wee heere dispatch
Yong good *Cornelia*, and you *Voltemar*
For bearers of these greetings to olde
Norway, giuing to you no further personall power
To businesse with the King,
Then those related articles do shew:
Farewell, and let your haste commend your dutie.

Gent. In this and all things will wee shew our dutie.

King. Wee doubt nothing, hartily farewele.
And now *Leartes*, what's the news with you?
You said you had a sute what i'st *Leartes*?

Lea. My gratious Lord, your fauorable licence,
Now that the funerall rites are all performed,

But   B 3

I.i.
160

165

170

175

I.ii.

28

30-3

35

40

43
50-1

I may haue leaue to go againe to *France*,
For though the fauour of your grace might ſtay mee,
Yet ſomething is there whiſpers in my hart,
Which makes my minde and ſpirits bend all for *France*.

 King Haue you your fathers leaue, *Leartes*?

 Cor. He hath, my lord, wrung from me a forced graunt,
And I beſeech you grant your Highneſſe leaue.

 Kiug With all our heart, *Leartes* fare thee well.

 Lear. I in all loue and dutie take my leaue.

 King. And now princely Sonne *Hamlet*, *Exit.*
What meanes theſe ſad and melancholy moodes?
For your intent going to *Wittenberg*,
Wee hold it moſt vnmeet and vnconuenient,
Being the Ioy and halfe heart of your mother.
Therefore let mee intreat you ſtay in Court,
All *Denmarkes* hope our cooſin and deareſt Sonne.

 Ham. My lord, ti's not the ſable ſute I weare:
No nor the teares that ſtill ſtand in my eyes,
Nor the diſtracted hauiour in the viſage,
Nor all together mixt with outward ſemblance,
Is equall to the ſorrow of my heart,
Him haue I loſt I muſt of force forgoe,
Theſe but the ornaments and ſutes of woe.

 King This ſhewes a louing care in you, Sonne *Hamlet*,
But you muſt thinke your father loſt a father,
That father dead, loſt his, and ſo ſhalbe vntill the
Generall ending. Therefore ceaſe laments,
It is a fault gainſt heauen, fault gainſt the dead,
A fault gainſt nature, and in reaſons
Common courſe moſt certaine,
None liues on earth, but hee is borne to die.

 Que. Let not thy mother looſe her praiers *Hamlet*,
Stay here with vs, go not to *Wittenberg*.

 Ham. I ſhall in all my beſt obay you madam.

 King Spoke like a kinde and a moſt louing Sonne,
And there's no health the King ſhall drinke to day,

But

But the great Canon to the clowdes shall tell
The rowse the King shall drinke vnto Prince *Hamlet*,

127

Exeunt all but Hamlet.

Ham. O that this too much grieu'd and sallied flesh

129

Would melt to nothing, or that the vniuersall

. 130

Globe of heauen would turne al to a Chaos!

138

O God, within two months; no not two : married,

Mine vncle : O let me not thinke of it,

151

My fathers brother : but no more like

My father, then I to *Hercules.*

*

Within two months, ere yet the salt of most

Vnrighteous teates had left their flushing

In her galled eyes : she married, O God, a beast

156

Deuoyd of reason would not haue made

150

Such speede : Frailtie, thy name is Woman,

. 146

Why she would hang on him, as if increase

143

Of appetite had growne by what it looked on.

144

O wicked wicked speede, to make such

156

Dexteritie to incestuous sheetes,

157

Ere yet the shooes were olde,

* 147

The which she followed my dead fathers corse

Like *Nyobe*, all teares : married, well it is not,

149

Nor it cannot come to good:

158

But breake my heart, for I must holde my tongue.

Enter Horatio *and* Marcellus.

Hor. Health to your Lordship.

Ham. I am very glad to see you, (*Horatio*) or I much

160

forget my selfe.

Hor. The same my Lord, and your poore seruant euer.

Ham. O my good friend, I change that name with you:

but what make you from *Wittenberg Horatio?*

165

Marcellus.

Marc. My good Lord.

Ham. I am very glad to see you, good euen sirs:

167

But what is your affaire in *Elsenoure?*

. 174

Weele teach you to drinke deepe ere you depart.

175

Hor.

I.ii.

Hor. A trowant difpofition, my good Lord.

Ham. Nor fhall you make mee trufter

Of your owne report againft your felfe:

Sir, I know you are no trowant:

But what is your affaire in *Elfenoure?*

   Hor. My good Lord, I came to fee your fathers funerall.

   Ham. O I pre thee do not mocke mee fellow ftudient,

I thinke it was to fee my mothers wedding.

   Hor. Indeede my Lord, it followed hard vpon.

   Ham. Thrift, thrift, *Horatio,* the funerall bak't meates

Did coldly furnifh forth the marriage tables,

Would I had met my deereft foe in heauen

Ere euer I had feene that day *Horatio,*

O my father, my father, me thinks I fee my father.

   Hor. Where my Lord?

   Ham. Why, in my mindes eye *Horatio.*

   Hor. I faw him once, he was a gallant King.

   Ham. He was a man, take him for all in all,

I fhall not looke vpon his like againe.

   Hor. My Lord, I thinke I faw him yefternight,

   Ham. Saw, who?

   Hor. My Lord, the King your father.

   Ham. Ha, ha, the King my father ke you.

   Hor. Ceafen your admiration for a while

With an attentiue eare, till I may deliuer,

Vpon the witneffe of thefe Gentlemen

This wonder to you.

   Ham. For Gods loue let me heare it.

   Hor. Two nights together had thefe Gentlemen,

Marcellus and *Bernardo,* on their watch,

In the dead vaft and middle of the night.

Beene thus incountered by a figure like your father,

Armed to poynt, exactly *Capapéa*

Appeeres before them thrife, he walkes

Before their weake and feare oppreffed eies

Within his tronchions length,

                      While

While they diſtilled almoſt to gelly,
With the act of feare ſtands dumbe,
And ſpeake not to him: this to mee
In dreadfull ſecreſie impart they did.
And I with them the third night kept the watch,
Where as they had deliuered forme of the thing,
Each part made true and good,
The Apparition comes: I knew your father,
Theſe handes are not more like.

    Ham. Tis very ſtrange.
    Hor. As I do liue, my honord lord, tis true,
And wee did thinke it right done,
In our dutie to let you know it.
    Ham. Where was this?
    Mar. My Lord, vpon the platforme where we watched.
    Ham. Did you not ſpeake to it?
    Hor. My Lord we did, but anſwere made it none,
Yet once me thought it was about to ſpeake,
And lifted vp his head to motion,
Like as he would ſpeake, but euen then
The morning cocke crew lowd, and in all haſte,
It ſhruncke in haſte away, and vaniſhed
Our ſight.
    Ham. Indeed, indeed ſirs, but this troubles me:
Hold you the watch to night?
    All We do my Lord.
    Ham. Armed ſay ye?
    All Armed my good Lord.
    Ham. From top to toe?
    All. My good Lord, from head to foote.
    Ham. Why then ſaw you not his face?
    Hor. O yes my Lord, he wore his beuer vp.
    Ham. How look't he, frowningly?
    Hor. A counntenance more in ſorrow than in anger.
    Ham. Pale, or red?
    Hor. Nay, verie pal

        C   *Ham.*

205
210
212
* 220
223
212
215
*
220
224
*
230

I.ii.

Ham. And fixt his eies vpon you.

Hor. Most constantly.

235 *Ham.* I would I had beene there.

Hor. It would a much amazed you.

Ham. Yea very like, very like, staid it long?

Hor. While one with moderate pace

Might tell a hundred.

Mar. O longer, longer.

Ham. His beard was grisseld, no.

240 *Hor.* It was as I haue seene it in his life,

A sable siluer.

Ham. I wil watch to night, perchance t'wil walke againe.

Hor. I warrant it will.

Ham. If it assume my noble fathers person,

245 Ile speake to it, if hell it selfe should gape,

And bid me hold my peace, Gentlemen,

If you haue hither consealed this sight,

Let it be tenible in your silence still,

And whatsoeuer else shall chance to night,

250 Giue it an vnderstanding, but no tongue,

I will requit your loues, so fare you well,

Vpon the platforme, twixt eleuen and twelue,

Ile visit you.

All. Our duties to your honor. *excunt.*

Ham. O your loues, your loues, as mine to you,

Farewell, my fathers spirit in Armes,

255 Well, all's not well. I doubt some foule play,

Would the night were come,

Till then, sit still my soule, foule deeds will rise

Though all the world orewhelme them to mens eies. *Exit.*

Enter Leartes and Ofelia.

I.iii.

1 *Leart.* My necessaries are inbarkt, I must aboord,

But ere I part, marke what I say to thee:

5 I see Prince *Hamlet* makes a shew of loue

10 Beware *Ofelia*, do not trust his vowes,

14 Perhaps he loues you now, and now his tongue,

Speakes

Speakes from his heart, but yet take heed my sister,
The Chariest maide is prodigall enough,
If she vnmaske hir beautie to the Moone.
Vertue it selfe scapes not calumnious thoughts,
Belieu't *Ofelia*, therefore keepe a loofe
Lest that he trip thy honor and thy fame.

   Ofel. Brother, to this I haue lent attentiue care,
And doubt not but to keepe my honour firme,
But my deere brother, do not you
Like to a cunning Sophister,
Teach me the path and ready way to heauen,
While you forgetting what is said to me,
Your selfe, like to a carelesse libertine
Doth giue his heart, his appetite at ful,
And little recks how that his honour dies.

   Lear. No, feare it not my deere *Ofelia*,
Here comes my father, occasion smiles vpon a second leaue.

      Enter Corambis.

   Cor. Yet here *Leartes*? aboord, aboord, for shame,
The winde sits in the shoulder of your saile,
And you are staid for, there my blessing with thee
And these few precepts in thy memory.
  " Be thou familiar, but by no meanes vulgare;
  " Those friends thou hast, and their adoptions tried,
  " Graple them to thee with a hoope of steele,
  " But do not dull the palme with entertaine,
  " Of euery new vnfleg'd courage,
  " Beware of entrance into a quarrell; but being in,
  " Beare it that the opposed may beware of thee,
  " Costly thy apparrell, as thy purse can buy.
  " But not exprest in fashion,
  " For the apparell oft proclaimes the man.
And they of *France* of the chiefe rancke and station
Are of a most select and generall chiefe in that:
  " This aboue all, to thy owne selfe be true,
And it must follow as the night the day,

          C 2   Thou

— laying his Hand
on Leartes Head

36
38
· 33-4

46
*
48

49

· 51
51
52-4

*
55

58
61

·

65

67
* 70

74
· 78

I.iii.

80   Thou canſt not then be falſe to any one,
      Farewel, my bleſſing with thee.

82-4   *Lear.* I humbly take my leaue, farewell *Ofelia*,
      And remember well what I haue ſaid to you.   *exis.*

      Ofel. It is already lock't within my hart,
86   And you your ſelfe ſhall keepe the key of it.

88   *Cor.* What i'ſt *Ofelia* he hath ſaide to you?

      Ofel. Somthing touching the prince *Hamlet.*

90-1   *Cor.* Mary wel thought on, t'is giuen me to vnderſtand,
92-3 *   That you haue bin too prodigall of your maiden preſence
      Vnto Prince Hamlet, if it be ſo,

95   As ſo tis giuen to mee, and that in waie of caution
      I muſt tell you; you do not vnderſtand your ſelfe

97   So well as befits my honor, and your credite.

99 •   *Ofel.* My lord, he hath made many tenders of his loue
100   to me.

103   *Cor.* Tenders, I, I, tenders you may call them.

114   *Ofel.* And withall, ſuch earneſt vowes.

        Cor. Springes to catch woodcocks,
*   What, do not I know when the blood doth burne,
117   How prodigall the tongue lends the heart vowes,
121   In briefe, be more ſcanter of your maiden preſence,
109   Or tendring thus you'l tender mee a foole.

136   *Ofel.* I ſhall obay my lord in all I may.

        Cor. *Ofelia*, receiue none of his letters,
      " For louers lines are ſnares to intrap the heart;
      " Refuſe his tokens, both of them are keyes
      To vnlocke Chaſtitie vnto Deſire;

135   Come in *Ofelia*, ſuch men often proue,
*   " Great in their wordes, but little in their loue.

        Ofel. I will my lord.   *exeunt.*

              Enter Hamlet, Horatio, *and* Marcellus.

I.iv.
1-2   *Ham.* The ayre bites ſhrewd; it is an eager and
      An nipping winde, what houre i'ſt?
2-3

3 •   *Hor.* I think it lacks of twelue,   *Sound Trumpets.*

        Mar. No, t'is ſtrucke.

                                          HORA.

Hor. Indeed I heard it not, what doth this mean my lord?

Ham. O the king doth wake to night, & takes his rowse,
Keepe waffel, and the swaggering vp-spring reeles,
drinks And as he dreames, his draughts of renish downe,
The kettle, drumme, and trumpet, thus bray out,
The triumphes of his pledge.

Hor. Is it a custome here?

Ham. I mary i'st and though I am
Natiue here, and to the maner borne,
It is a custome, more honourd in the breach,
Then in the obseruance.

Enter the Ghost.

Hor. Looke my Lord, it comes.

Ham. Angels and Ministers of grace defend vs,
Be thou a spirite of health, or goblin damn'd,
Bring with thee ayres from heanen, or blasts from hell:
Be thy intents wicked or charitable,
Thou commest in such questionable shape,
That I will speake to thee,
Ile call thee *Hamlet*, King, Father, Royall Dane,
O answere mee, let mee not burst in ignorance,
But say why thy canonizd bones hearsed in death
Haue burst their ceremonies: why thy Sepulcher,
In which wee saw thee quietly interr'd,
Hath burst his ponderous and marble Iawes,
To cast thee vp againe: what may this meane,
That thou, dead corse, againe in compleate steele,
Reuissets thus the glimses of the Moone,
Making night hideous, and we fooles of nature,
So horridely to shake our disposition,
With thoughts beyond the reaches of our soules?
Say, speake, wherefore, what may this meane?

Hor. It beckons you, as though it had something
To impart to you alone.

Mar. Looke with what courteous action
It waues you to a more remoued ground,

But

5-7

10

*

16

38

• 40

*

45

• 50

* 55

• 60

I.iv.

But do not go with it.

   Hor. No, by no meanes my Lord.

63
69
71 .

   Ham. It will not speake, then will I follow it.

   Hor. What if it tempt you toward the flood my Lord.

That beckles ore his bace, into the sea,

And there assume some other horrible shape,

Which might depriue your soueraigntie of reason,

And driue you into madnesse : thinke of it.

74
78-9
80 *
84

   Ham. Still am I called, go on, ile follow thee.

   Hor. My Lord, you shall not go.

   Ham. Why what should be the feare?

I do not set my life at a pinnes fee,

And for my soule, what can it do to that?

Being a thing immortall, like it selfe,

88 .
81

Go on, ile follow thee.

   Mar. My Lord be rulde, you shall not goe.

   Ham. My fate cries out, and makes each pety Artiue

As hardy as the Nemeon Lyons nerue,

85 *

Still am I cald, vnhand me gentlemen;

By heauen ile make a ghost of him that lets me,

Away I say, go on, ile follow thee.

87
90
89
91 .
I.v.

   Hor. He waxeth desperate with imagination.

   Mar. Something is rotten in the state of *Denmarke.*

   Hor. Haue after; to what issue will this sort?

   Mar. Lets follow, tis not fit thus to obey him.   *exit.*

      Enter Ghost and Hamlet.

1
2
2
9 *

   Ham. Ile go no farther, whither wilt thou leade me?

   Ghost Marke me.

   Ham. I will.

   Ghost I am thy fathers spirit, doomd for a time

To walke the night, and all the day

Confinde in flaming fire,

13
4 .
5-6

Till the foule crimes done in my dayes of Nature

Are purged and burnt away.

   Ham. Alas poore Ghost.

   Ghost Nay pitty me not, but to my vnfolding

                                 Lend

Lend thy liſtning eare, but that I am forbid

To tell the ſecrets of my priſon houſe

I would a tale vnfold, whoſe lighteſt word

Would harrow vp thy ſoule, freeze thy yong blood,

Make thy two eyes like ſtars ſtart from their ſpheres,

Thy knotted and combined locks to part,

And each particular haire to ſtand on end

Like quils vpon the fretfull Porpentine,

But this ſame blazon muſt not be, to eares of fleſh and blood

Hamlet, if euer thou didſt thy deere father loue.

   Ham. O God.

   Gho. Reuenge his foule, and moſt vnnaturall murder :

   Ham. Murder.

   Ghoſt Yea, murder in the higheſt degree,

As in the leaſt tis bad,

But mine moſt foule, beaſtly, and vnnaturall.

   Ham. Haſte me to knowe it, that with wings as ſwift as

meditation, or the thought of it, may ſweepe to my reuenge.

   Ghoſt O I finde thee apt, and duller ſhouldſt thou be

Then the fat weede which rootes it ſelfe in eaſe

On *Lethe* wharffe : briefe let me be.

Tis giuen out, that ſleeping in my orchard,

A Serpent ſtung me ; ſo the whole eare of *Denmarke*

Is with a forged Proſſes of my death rankely abuſde:

But know thou noble Youth : he that did ſting

Thy fathers heart, now weares his Crowne.

   Ham. O my prophetike ſoule, my vncle! my vncle!

   Ghoſt Yea he, that inceſtuous wretch, wonne to his will

O wicked will, and gifts! that haue the power   (with gifts,

So to ſeduce my moſt ſeeming vertuous Queene,

But vertne, as it neuer will be moued,

Though Lewdneſſe court it in a ſhape of heauen,

So Luſt, though to a radiant angle linckt,

Would ſate it ſelfe from a celeſtiall bedde,

And prey on garbage : but ſoft, me thinkes

I ſent the mornings ayre, briefe let me be,

                        Sleeping

5-13
15
.
.
20
*
25
.
30
*
33
35
.
40-1
42 3
* 45-6
53
55
.

I.v.

60 Sleeping within my Orchard, my cuſtome alwayes
In the after-noone, vpon my ſecure houre
Thy vncle came, with iuyce of Hebona
In a viall, and through the porches of my eares
65 Did powre the leaprous diſtilment, whoſe effect
Hold ſuch an enmitie with blood of man,
67 That ſwift as quickeſilner, it poſteth through
70 The naturall gates and allies of the body,
69 * And turnes the thinne and wholeſome blood
73-1 Like eager dropings into milke.
74 And all my ſmoothe body, barked, and tetterd ouer.
Thus was I ſleeping by a brothers hand
75-8 Of Crowne, of Queene, of life, of dignitie
At once depriued, no reckoning made of,
78 But ſent vnto my graue,
80 With all my accompts and ſinnes vpon my head,
O horrible, moſt horrible!
81 *Ham.* O God!
84-5 * *ghoſt* If thou haſt nature in thee, beare it not,
But howſoeuer, let not thy heart
Conſpire againſt thy mother aught,
Leaue her to heauen,
87 And to the burthen that her conſcience beares.
90 I muſt be gone, the Glo-worme ſhewes the Martin
To be neere, and gins to pale his vneffectuall fire:
Hamlet adue, adue, adue: remember me. *Exit*
Ham. O all you hoſte of heauen! O earth, what elſe?
93-5 And ſhall I couple hell; remember thee?
96-8 Yes thou poore Ghoſt; from the tables
100 * Of my memorie, ile wipe away all ſawes of Bookes,
99 All triuiall fond conceites
101 That euer youth, or elſe obſeruance noted,
102 And thy remembrance, all alone ſhall ſit.
104-5 Yes, yes, by heauen, a damnd pernitious villaine,
Murderons, bawdy, ſmiling damned villaine,
(My tables) meet it is I ſet it downe,

That

That one may smile, and smile, and be a villayne;
At least I am sure, it may be so in *Denmarke*.
So vncle, there you are, there you are.   110
Now to the words; it is adue adue : remember me,   101-1
Soe t'is enough I haue sworne.

 Hor. My lord, my lord.   *Enter. Horatio,*
 Mar. Lord Hamlet.   *and Marcellus.*   113
 Hor. Ill, lo, lo, ho, ho.   115
 Mar. Ill, lo, lo, so, ho, so, come boy, come.   116
 Hor. Heauens secure him.   * 113
 Mar. How i'st my noble lord?   117
 Hor. What news my lord?
 Ham. O wonderfull, wonderful.
 Hor. Good my lord tel it.
 Ham. No not I, you'l reueale it.
 Hor. Not I my Lord by heauen.
 Mar. Nor I my Lord.   120
 Ham. How say you then? would hart of man
Once thinke it? but you'l be secret.
 Both. I by heauen, my lord.   *
 Ham. There's neuer a villaine dwelling in all *Denmarke*,
But hee's an arrant knaue.
 Hor. There need no Ghost come from the graue to tell   125
you this.
 Ham. Right, you are in the right, and therefore
I holde it meet without more circumstance at all,
Wee shake hands and part; you as your busines
And desiers shall leade you : for looke you,
Euery man hath busines, and desires, such   * 130
As it is, and for my owne poore parte, ile go pray.
 Hor. These are but wild and wherling words, my Lord.
 Ham. I am sory they offend you; hartely, yes faith hartily.
 Hor. Ther's no offence my Lord.   135
 Ham. Yes by Saint *Patrike* but there is *Horatio*,
And much offence too, touching this vision,
It is an honest ghost, that let mee tell you,

     D   For

For your desires to know what is betweene vs,
Or emaister it as you may:
And now kind frends, as yon are frends,
Schollers and gentlmen,
Grant mee one poore request.

 Both. What ist my Lord?
 Ham. Neuer make known what you haue seene to night
 Both. My lord, we will not.
 Ham. Nay but sweare.
 Hor. In faith my Lord not I.
 Mar. Nor I my Lord in faith.
 Ham. Nay vpon my sword, indeed vpon my sword.
 Gho. Sweare.

    The Gost vnder the stage.

 Ham. Ha, ha, come you here, this fellow in the sellerige,
Here consent to sweare.
 Hor. Propose the oth my Lord.
 Ham. Neuer to speake what you haue seene to night,
Sweare by my sword.
 Gost. Sweare.
 Ham. Hic & vbique, nay then weele shift our ground:
Come hither Gentlemen, and lay your handes
Againe vpon this sword, neuer to speake
Of that which you haue seene, sweare by my sword.
 Ghost Sweare.
 Ham. Well said old Mole, can'st worke in the earth?
so fast, a worthy Pioner, once more remoue.
 Hor. Day and night, but this is wondrous strange.
 Ham. And therefore as a stranger giue it welcome,
There are more things in heauen and earth *Horatio,*
Then are Dream't of, in your philosophie,
But come here, as before you neuer shall
How strange or odde soere I beare my selfe,
As I perchance hereafter shall thinke meet,
To put an Anticke disposition on,
That you at such times seeing me, neuer shall

           With

With Armes, incombred thus, or this head shake,
Or by pronouncing some vndoubtfull phrase,
As well well, wee know, or wee could and if we would,
Or there be, and if they might, or such ambiguous:
Giuing out to note, that you know aught of mee,
This not to doe, so grace, and mercie
At your most need helpe you, sweare
   Ghost. sweare.
   Ham. Rest, rest, perturbed spirit: so gentlemen,
In all my loue I do commend mee to you,
And what so poore a man as *Hamlet* may,
To pleasure you, God willing shall not want,
Nay come lett's go together,
But stil your fingers on your lippes I pray,
The time is out of ioynt, O cursed spite,
That euer I was borne to set it right,
Nay come lett's go together.   *Exeunt.*
   Enter Corambis, and Montano.   *Now call'd Polonius.*
   Cor. Montano, here, these letters to my sonne,
And this same mony with my blessing to him,
And bid him ply his learning good *Montano*.
   Mon. I will my lord.
   Cor. You shall do very well *Montano*, to say thus,
I knew the gentleman, or know his father,
To inquire the manner of his life,
As thus; being amongst his acquaintance,
You may say, you saw him at such a time, marke you mee,
At game, or drincking, swearing, or drabbing,
You may go so farre.
   Mon. My lord, that will impeach his reputation.
   Cor. I faith not a whit, no not a whit,
Now happely hee closeth with you in the consequence,
As you may bridle it not disparage him a iote.
What was I about to say,
   Mon. He closeth with him in the consequence.
   Cor. I, you say right, he closeth with him thus,
         D 2   This

I.v.

175

·

180-1

*

185

·

190

II.i.

1

* 1

73

2

3

14

· 4-5

56

24-5

*

28

45

28

51

· 52

54

II.i.

This will hee say, let mee see what hee will say,

54-6 Mary this, I saw him yesterday, or tother day,
57-8 Or then, or at such a time, a dicing,
58-9 Or at Tennis, I or drincking drunke, or entring
60-1 Of a howse of lightnes viz. brothell,
64 Thus sir do wee that know the world, being men of reach,
66 By indirections, finde directions forth,
68 And so shall you my sonne; you ha me, ha you not?

 Mon. I haue my lord.

69 *Cor.* Wel, fare you well, commend mee to him.

 Mon. I will my lord.

71 *Cor.* And bid him ply his musicke

 Mon. My lord I wil.   *exit.*

   Enter, Ofelia.

74 *Cor.* Farewel, how now *Ofelia*, what's the news with you?

75 *Ofe.* O my deare father, such a change in nature,

So great an alteration in a Prince,

So pitifull to him, fearefull to mee,

A maidens eye ne're looked on.

 Cor. Why what's the matter my *Ofelia*?

74-6 *Of.* O yong Prince *Hamlet*, the only floure of *Denmark*,
78 Hee is bereft of all the wealth he had,

The Iewell that ador'nd his feature most

Is filcht and stolne away, his wit's bereft him,

77 Hee found mee walking in the gallery all alone,
84-2 There comes hee to mee, with a distracted looke,
80 His garters lagging downe, his shooes vntide,
90 And fixt his eyes so stedfast on my face,

As if they had vow'd, this is their latest obiect.

87 Small while he stoode, but gripes me by the wrist,

And there he holdes my pulse till with a sigh

He doth vnclaspe his holde, and parts away

96 Silent, as is the mid time of the night:

100 And as he went, his eie was still on mee,

97 For thus his head ouer his shoulder looked,

He seemed to finde the way without his eies:

           For

For out of doores he went without their helpe,
And so did leaue me.

 Cor. Madde for thy loue,
What haue you giuen him any crosse wordes of late?

 Ofelia I did repell his letters, deny his gifts,
As you did charge me.

 Cor. Why that hath made him madde:
By heau'n t'is as proper for our age to cast
Beyond our selues, as t'is for the yonger sort
To leaue their wantonnesse. Well, I am sory
That I was so rash: but what remedy?
Lets to the King, this madnesse may prooue,
Though wilde a while, yet more true to thy loue. *exeunt.*
 Enter King and Queene, Rossencraft, and Gilderstone.

 King Right noble friends, that our deere cosin Hamlet
Hath lost the very heart of all his sence,
It is most right, and we most sory for him:
Therefore we doe desire, euen as you tender
Our care to him, and our great loue to you,
That you will labour but to wring from him
The cause and ground of his distemperancie.
Doe this, the king of *Denmarke* shal be thankefull.

 Ros. My Lord, whatsoeuer lies within our power
Your maiestie may more commaund in wordes
Then vse perswasions to your liege men, bound
By loue, by duetie, and obedience.

 Guil. What we may doe for both your Maiesties
To know the griefe troubles the Prince your sonne,
We will indeuour all the best we may,
So in all duetie doe we take our leaue.

 King Thankes Guilderstone, and gentle Rossencraft.

 Que. Thankes Rossencraft, and gentle Gilderstone.
  Enter Corambis and Ofelia.

 Cor. My Lord, the Ambassadors are ioyfully
Return'd from *Norway.*

 King Thou still hast beene the father of good news.
   D 3   *Cor.*

II.i.
99
102
107
•109
108
110
114
115-6
*117-1
111
117

II.ii.
•1-5
5
10
*15-6
26
28
•29
*
34
33
40
•

II.ii.

Cor. Haue I my Lórd? I aſſure your grace,
I holde my duetie as I holde my life,
45 Both to my God, and to my ſoueraigne King:
And I beleeue, or elſe this braine of mine
Hunts not the traine of policie ſo well
As it had wont to doe, but I haue found
The very depth of Hamlets lunacie.
50   *Queene* God graunt he hath.
        Enter the Ambaſſadors.
59 *   *King* Now *Voltemar*, what from our brother *Norway*?
    Volt. Moſt faire returnes of greetings and deſires,
Vpon our firſt he ſent forth to ſuppreſſe
His nephews leuies, which to him appear'd
To be a preparation gainſt the Polacke:
65 But better look't into, he truely found
It was againſt your Highneſſe, whereat grieued,
That ſo his ſickeneſſe, age, and impotence,
Was falſely borne in hand, ſends out arreſts
On *Fortenbraſſe*, which he in briefe obays,
Receiues rebuke from *Norway*: and in fine,
70 Makes vow before his vncle, neuer more
To giue the aſſay of Armes againſt your Maieſtie,
Whereon olde *Norway* ouercome with ioy,
Giues him three thouſand crownes in annuall fee,
And his Commiſſion to employ thoſe ſouldiers,
75 So leuied as before, againſt the Polacke,
With an intreaty heerein further ſhewne,
That it would pleaſe you to giue quiet paſſe
Through your dominions, for that enterpriſe
* On ſuch regardes of ſafety and allowances
As therein are ſet downe.
80   *King* It likes vs well, and at fit time and leaſure
Weele reade and anſwere theſe his Articles,
Meane time we thanke you for your well
Tooke labour: go to your reſt, at night weele feaſt togither:
Right welcome home.   *exeunt Ambaſſadors.*

                                        Cor.

Cor. This busines is very well dispatched.   85
Now my Lord, touching the yong Prince Hamlet,
Certaine it is that hee is madde: mad let vs grant him then: 92-3
Now to know the cause of this effect,   101
Or else to say the cause of this defect,
For this effect defectiue comes by cause.   103
    Queene Good my Lord be briefe.   95
    Cor. Madam I will: my Lord, I haue a daughter,   96
Haue while shee's mine: for that we thinke   106
Is surest, we often loose: now to the Prince.   *
My Lord, but note this letter,
The which my daughter in obedience   107
Deliuer'd to my handes.   108
    King Reade it my Lord.
    Cor. Marke my Lord.   . 108
Doubt that in earth is fire,   116
Doubt that the starres doe moue,
Doubt trueth to be a liar,
But doe not doubt I loue.   119
To the beautifull *Ofelia* :   * 109-10
Thine euer the most vnhappy Prince *Hamlet.*   123-4
My Lord, what doe you thinke of me?   129
I, or what might you thinke when I sawe this?   131-2
    King As of a true friend and a most louing subiect.   130
    Cor. I would be glad to prooue so.   . 131
Now when I saw this letter, thus I bespake my maiden: 140
Lord *Hamlet* is a Prince out of your starre,   141
And one that is vnequall for your loue:
Therefore I did commaund her refuse his letters,   142
Deny his tokens, and to absent her selfe.   * 144-3
Shee as my childe obediently obey'd me.   145
Now since which time, seeing his loue thus cros'd,   146
Which I tooke to be idle, and but sport,
He straitway grew into a melancholy,   147
From that vnto a fast, then vnto distraction,   . 147
Then into a sadnesse, from that vnto a madnesse,   147
               And

And so by continuance, and weakenesse of the braine
Into this frensie, which now possesseth him:
And if this be not true, take this from this.

King Thinke you t'is so?

Cor. How? so my Lord, I would very faine know
That thing that I haue saide t'is so, positiuely,
And it hath fallen out otherwise.
Nay, if circumstances leade me on,
Ile finde it out, if it were hid
As deepe as the centre of the earth.

King. how should wee trie this same?

Cor. Mary my good lord thus,
The Princes walke is here in the galery,
There let *Ofelia,* walke vntill hee comes:
Your selfe and I will stand close in the study,
There shall you heare the effect of all his hart,
And if it proue any otherwise then loue,
Then let my censure faile an other time.

King. see where hee comes poring vppon a booke.

Enter Hamlet.

Cor. Madame, will it please your grace
To leaue vs here?

Que. With all my hart.   *exit.*

Cor. And here *Ofelia,* reade you on this booke,
And walke aloofe, the King shal be vnseene.

Ham. To be, or not to be, I there's the point,
To Die, to sleepe, is that all? I all:
No, to sleepe, to dreame, I mary there it goes,
For in that dreame of death, when wee awake,
And borne before an euerlasting Iudge,
From whence no passenger euer retur'nd,
The vndiscouered country, at whose sight
The happy smile, and the accursed damn'd.
But for this, the ioyfull hope of this,
Whol'd beare the scornes and flattery of the world,
Scorned by the right rich, the rich curssed of the poore?

                                        The

The widow being oppreſſed,the orphan wrong'd,
The taſte of hunger, or a tirants raigne,
And thouſand more calamities beſides,
To grunt and ſweate vnder this weary life,
When that he may his full *Quietus* make,
With a bare bodkin, who would this indure,
But for a hope of ſomething after death?
Which puſſes the braine, and doth confound the ſence,
Which makes vs rather beare thoſe euilles we haue,
Than flie to others that we know not of.
I that,O this conſcience makes cowardes of vs all,
Lady in thy orizons, be all my ſinnes remembred.

   Ofel. My Lord, I haue ſought opportunitie,which now
I haue,to redeliuer to your worthy handes, a ſmall remembrance,ſuch tokens which I haue receiued of you.

   Ham. Are you faire?

   Ofel. My Lord.

   Ham. Are you honeſt?

   Ofel. What meanes my Lord?

   Ham. That if you be faire and honeſt,
Your beauty ſhould admit no diſcourſe to your honeſty.

   Ofel. My Lord, can beauty haue better priuiledge than
with honeſty?

   Ham. Yea mary may it; for Beauty may transforme
Honeſty, from what ſhe was into a bawd:
Then Honeſty can transforme Beauty:
This was ſometimes a Paradox,
But now the time giues it ſcope.
I neuer gaue you nothing.

   Ofel. My Lord, you know right well you did,
And with them ſuch earneſt vowes of loue,
As would haue moou'd the ſtonieſt breaſt aliue,
But now too true I finde,
Rich giftes waxe poore, when giuers grow vnkinde.

   Ham. I neuer loued you.

   Ofel. You made me beleeue you did.

                    E   *Ham.*

III.i.

118   *Ham.* O thou shouldst not a beleeued me!

122   Go to a Nunnery goe, why shouldst thou
      Be a breeder of sinners? I am my selfe indifferent honest,
      But I could accuse my selfe of such crimes

125 ·   It had beene better my mother had ne're borne me,
      O I am very prowde, ambitious, disdainefull,
      With more sinnes at my becke, then I haue thoughts

128-9   To put them in, what should such fellowes as I
      Do, crawling betweene heauen and earth?

132-1 *   To a Nunnery goe, we are arrant knaues all,

131-2   Beleeue none of vs, to a Nunnery goe:
        Ofel. O heauens secure him!

132-3   *Ham.* Wher's thy father?
        Ofel. At home my lord.

135 ·   *Ham.* For Gods sake let the doores be shut on him,
      He may play the foole no where but in his
      Owne house: to a Nunnery goe.
        Ofel. Help him good God.
        Ham. If thou dost marry, Ile giue thee

*   This plague to thy dowry:

140   Be thou as chaste as yce, as pure as snowe,

141-2   Thou shalt not scape calumny, to a Nunnery goe.
        Ofel. Alas, what change is this?

142   *Ham.* But if thou wilt needes marry, marry a foole,
·   For wisemen know well enough,

145   What monsters you make of them, to a Nunnery goe.

147   *Ofel.* Pray God restore him.
        Ham. Nay, I haue heard of your paintings too,
      God hath giuen you one face,

*   And you make your selues another,

150   You sig, and you amble, and you nickname Gods creatures,
      Making your wantonnesse, your ignorance,
      A pox, t is scuruy, Ile no more of it,
      It hath made me madde : Ile no more marriages,
·   All that are married but one, shall liue,

157   The rest shall keepe as they are, to a Nunnery goe,

                           To

To a Nunnery goe.   *exit.*

Ofe. Great God of heauen, what a quicke change is this?
The Courtier, Scholler, Souldier, all in him,
All dasht and splinterd thence, O woe is me,
To a seene what I haue seene, see what I see.   *exit.*

King Loue? No, no, that's not the cause,   *Enter King and*
Some deeper thing it is that troubles him.   *Corambis.*

Cor. Wel, something it is: my Lord, content you a while,
I will my selfe goe feele him: let me worke,
Ile try him euery way: see where he comes,
Send you those Gentlemen, let me alone
To finde the depth of this, away, be gone.   *exit King.*
Now my good Lord, do you know me?   *Enter Hamlet.*

Ham. Yea very well, y'are a fishmonger.

Cor. Not I my Lord.

Ham. Then sir, I would you were so honest a man,
For to be honest, as this age goes,
Is one man to be pickt out of tenne thousand.

Cor. What doe you reade my Lord?

Ham. Wordes, wordes.

Cor. What's the matter my Lord?

Ham. Betweene who?

Cor. I meane the matter you reade my Lord.

Ham. Mary most vile heresie:
For here the Satyricall Satyre writes,
That olde men haue hollow eyes, weake backes,
Grey beardes, pittifull weake hammes, gowty legges,
All which sir, I most potently beleeue not:
For sir, your selfe shalbe olde as I am,
If like a Crabbe, you could goe backeward.

Cor. How pregnant his replies are, and full of wit:
Yet at first he tooke me for a fishmonger:
All this comes by loue, the vemencie of loue,
And when I was yong, I was very idle,
And suffered much extasie in loue, very neere this:
Will you walke out of the aire my Lord?

                    E 2   *Ham.*

Ham. Into my graue.

Cor. By the masse that's out of the aire indeed,
Very shrewd answers,
My lord I will take my leaue of you.

            Enter Gilderstone, and Rossencraft.

Ham. You can take nothing from me sir,
I will more willingly part with all,
Olde doating foole.

    Cor, You seeke Prince Hamlet, see, there he is. *exit.*

    Gil. Health to your Lordship.

    Ham. What, Gilderstone, and Rossencraft,
Welcome kinde Schoole-fellowes to *Elsanoure.*

    Gil. We thanke your Grace, and would be very glad
You were as when we were at *Wittenberg.*

    Ham. I thanke you, but is this visitation free of
Your selues, or were you not sent for?
Tell me true, come, I know the good King and Queene
Sent for you, there is a kinde of confession in your eye:
Come, I know you were sent for.

    Gil. What say you?

    Ham. Nay then I see how the winde sits,
Come, you were sent for.

    Ross. My lord, we were, and willingly if we might,
Know the cause and ground of your discontent.

    Ham. Why I want preferment.

    Ross. I thinke not so my lord.

    Ham. Yes faith, this great world you see contents me not,
No nor the spangled heauens, nor earth, nor sea,
No nor Man that is so glorious a creature,
Contents not me, no nor woman too, though you laugh.

    Gil. My lord, we laugh not at that.

    Ham. Why did you laugh then,
When I said, Man did not content mee?

    Gil. My Lord, we laughed, when you said, Man did not
content you.
What entertainement the Players shall haue,

                         We

211
217-8

220
223
224
229

281-4
282
284-90
289
288-9
300
301

303

310
312
321
322
324-5

We boorded them a the way : they are comming to you.

   Ham. Players ,what Players be they?

   Roff. My Lord, the Tragedians of the Citty,

Those that you tooke delight to fee fo often.   (ftie?

   Ham. How comes it that they trauell? Do they grow re-

   Gil. No my Lord, their reputation holds as it was wont.

   Ham. How then?

   Gil. Yfaith my Lord, noueltie carries it away,

For the principall publike audience that

Came to them, are turned to priuate playes,

And to the humour of children.

   Ham. I doe not greatly wonder of it,

For thofe that would make mops and moes

At my vncle, when my father liued,

Now giue a hundred, two hundred pounds

For his picture : but they fhall be welcome,

He that playes the King fhall haue tribute of me,

The ventrous Knight fhall vfe his foyle and target,

The louer fhall figh gratis,

The clowne fhall make them laugh   (for't,

That are tickled in the lungs , or the blanke verfe fhall halt

And the Lady fhall haue leaue to fpeake her minde freely.

    The Trumpets found,   *Enter Corambis.*

Do you fee yonder great baby?

He is not yet out of his fwadling clowts.

   Gil. That may be, for they fay an olde man

Is twice a childe.   (Players,

   Ham. Ile prophecie to you, hee comes to tell mee a the

You fay true, a monday laft, t'was fo indeede.

   Cor. My lord, I haue news to tell you.

   Ham. My Lord, I haue newes to tell you:

When *Roffios* was an Actor in *Rome.*

   Cor. The Actors are come hither, my lord.

   Ham. Buz, buz.

   Cor. The beft Actors in Chriftendome,

Either for Comedy, Tragedy, Hiftorie, Paftorall,

       Paftorall

II.ii.

330-1
339
342
341
• 343-53
353
352
347

*

354
380

•

383-32
333

335
* 337
339
338

400
• 401
403

405

*

410

412
• 415

Paſtorall, Hiſtoricall, Hiſtoricall, Comicall,
Comicall hiſtoricall, Paſtorall, Tragedy hiſtoricall:
Seneca cannot be too heauy, nor *Plato* too light:
For the law hath writ thoſe are the onely men.

    Ha. O *Iepha* Iudge of *Iſrael!* what a treaſure hadſt thou?
    Cor. Why what a treaſure had he my lord?
    Ham. Why one faire daughter, and no more,
The which he loued paſsing well.
    Cor. A, ſtil harping a my daughter! well my Lord,
If you call me *Iepha*, I haue a daughter that
I loue paſsing well.
    Ham. Nay that followes not.
    Cor. What followes then my Lord?
    Ham. Why by lot, or God wot, or as it came to paſse,
And ſo it was, the firſt verſe of the godly Ballet
Wil tel you all: for look you where my abridgement comes:
Welcome maiſters, welcome all,   *Enter players.*
What my olde friend, thy face is vallanced
Since I ſaw thee laſt, com'ſt thou to beard me in *Denmarke?*
My yong lady and miſtris, burlady but your   (you were:
Ladiſhip is growne by the altitude of a chopine higher than
Pray God ſir your voyce, like a peece of vncurrant
Golde, be not crack't in the ring: come on maiſters,
Weele euen too't, like French Falconers,
Flie at any thing we ſee, come, a taſte of your
Quallitie, a ſpeech, a paſsionate ſpeech.
    Players What ſpeech my good lord?
    Ham. I heard thee ſpeake a ſpeech once,
But it was neuer acted: or if it were,
Neuer aboue twice, for as I remember,
It pleaſed not the vulgar, it was cauiary
To the million : but to me
And others, that receiued it in the like kinde,
Cried in the toppe of their iudgements, an excellent play,
Set downe with as great modeſtie as cunning:
One ſaid there was no ſallets in the lines to make thē ſauory,
                                              But

But called it an honest methode, as wholesome as sweete.   475

Come, a speech in it I chiefly remember   467

Was *Æneas* tale to *Dido*,

And then especially where he talkes of Princes slaughter,

If it liue in thy memory beginne at this line,   • 470

Let me see.

The rugged *Pyrrus*, like th'arganian beast:

No t'is not so, it begins with *Pirrus*:   473

O I haue it.

The rugged *Pirrus*, he whose sable armes,   * 474

Blacke as his purpose did the night resemble,

When he lay couched in the ominous horse,

Hath now his blacke and grimme complexion smeered

With Heraldry more dismall, head to foote,

Now is he totall guise, horridely tricked

With blood of fathers, mothers, daughters, sonnes,

Back't and imparched in calagulate gore,   481-4

Rifted in earth and fire, olde grandsire *Pryam* seekes: 486

So goe on.   (accent.

   Cor. Afore God, my Lord, well spoke, and with good   *

   Play. Anone he finds him striking too short at Greeks,   490

His antike sword rebellious to his Arme,

Lies where it falles, vnable to resist.   492

Pyrrus at *Pryam* driues, but all in rage,   494

Strikes wide, but with the whiffe and winde

Of his fell sword, th'vnnerued father falles.   •

   Cor. Enough my friend, t'is too long.   496

   Ham. It shall to the Barbers with your beard: 520

A pox, hee's for a ligge, or a tale of bawdry,

Or else he sleepes, come on to *Hecuba*, come.   *

   Play. But who, O who had seene the mobled Queene?   524

   Cor. Mobled Queene is good, faith very good.   526

   Play. All in the alarum and feare of death rose vp,   532

And o're her weake and all ore-teeming loynes, a blancket   531

And a kercher on that head, where late the diademe stoode,   • 529-30

Who this had seene with tongue inuenom'd speech,   533

                       Would

Would treaſon haue pronounced,
For if the gods themſelues had ſeene her then,
When ſhe ſaw *Pirrus* with malitious ſtrokes,
Mincing her husbandes limbs,
It would haue made milch the burning eyes of heauen,
And paſſion in the gods.

 Cor. Looke my lord if he hath not changde his colour,
And hath teares in his eyes: no more good heart, no more.

 Ham. T'is well, t'is very well, I pray my lord,
Will you ſee the Players well beſtowed,
I tell you they are the Chronicles
And briefe abſtracts of the time,
After your death I can tell you,
You were better haue a bad Epiteeth,
Then their ill report while you liue.

 Cor. My lord, I will vſe them according to their deſerts.

 Ham. O farre better man, vſe euery man after his deſerts,
Then who ſhould ſcape whipping?
Vſe them after your owne honor and dignitie,
The leſſe they deſerue, the greater credit's yours.

 Cor. Welcome my good fellowes.   *exit.*

 Ham. Come hither maiſters, can you not play the murder of *Gonſago?*

 players Yes my Lord.

 Ham. And could'ſt not thou for a neede ſtudy me
Some dozen or ſixteene lines,
Which I would ſet downe and inſert?

 players Yes very eaſily my good Lord.

 Ham. T'is well, I thanke you: follow that lord:
And doe you heare ſirs? take heede you mocke him not.
Gentlemen, for your kindnes I thanke you,
And for a time I would deſire you leaue me.

 Gil. Our loue and duetie is at your commaund.

    Exeunt all but Hamlet.

 Ham. Why what a dunghill idiote ſlaue am I?
Why theſe Players here draw water from eyes:

             For

For Hecuba, why what is Hecuba to him, or he to Hecuba? 584-5
What would he do and if he had my loſſe? 586-7
His father murdred, and a Crowne bereft him,
He would turne all his teares to droppes of blood, 588
Amaze the ſtanders by with his laments, •589-91
Strike more then wonder in the iudiciall eares,
Confound the ignorant, and make mute the wiſe, 591
Indeede his paſſion would be generall.
Yet I like to an aſſe and Iohn a Dreames, 593-5
Hauing my father murdred by a villaine, *596-8
Stand ſtill, and let it paſſe, why ſure I am a coward: 596-8
Who pluckes me by the beard, or twites my noſe, 600-1
Giue's me the lie i'th throate downe to the lungs, 601-2
Sure I ſhould take it, or elſe I haue no gall, 604-5
Or by this I ſhould a fatted all the region kites •606-7
With this ſlaues offell, this damned villaine,
Treacherous, bawdy, murderous villaine: 609
Why this is braue, that I the ſonne of my deare father, 611-2
Should like a ſcalion, like a very drabbe 616-5
Thus raile in wordes. About my braine, *614-7
I haue heard that guilty creatures ſitting at a play,
Hath, by the very cunning of the ſcene, confeſt a murder 619
Committed long before.
This ſpirit that I haue ſeene may be the Diuell, 627-8
And out of my weakeneſſe and my melancholy, •630
As he is very potent with ſuch men,
Doth ſeeke to damne me, I will haue ſounder proofes,
The play's the thing,
Wherein I'le catch the conſcience of the King. *exit.* 634

Enter the King, Queene, and Lordes. * III.i.

King Lordes, can you by no meanes finde 1
The cauſe of our ſonne Hamlets lunacie? 2-4
You being ſo neere in loue, euen from his youth,
Me thinkes ſhould gaine more than a ſtranger ſhould.

F   Gil

III.i.

5-6
8
9-10
18 .
20
20-1
22-3
24
26 *

28

*

*

188-9
190
192-3
191 *

*

Gil. My lord, we haue done all the best we could,
To wring from him the cause of all his griefe,
But still he puts vs off, and by no meanes
Would make an answere to that we exposde.

Ross. Yet was he something more inclin'd to mirth
Before we left him, and I take it,
He hath giuen order for a play to night,
At which he craues your highnesse company.

King With all our heart, it likes vs very well:
Gentlemen, seeke still to increase his mirth,
Spare for no cost, our coffers shall be open,
And we vnto your selues will still be thankefull.

Both In all wee can, be sure you shall commaund.

Queene Thankes gentlemen, and what the Queene of
May pleasure you, be sure you shall not want. (*Denmarke*

Gil. Weele once againe vnto the noble Prince.

King Thanks to you both: Gertred you'l see this play.

Queene My lord I will, and it ioyes me at the soule
He is inclin'd to any kinde of mirth.

Cor. Madame, I pray be ruled by me:
And my good Soueraigne, giue me leaue to speake,
We cannot yet finde out the very ground
Of his distemperance, therefore
I holde it meete, if so it please you,
Else they shall not meete, and thus it is.

King What i'st *Corambis*?   (done,

Cor. Mary my good lord this, soone when the sports are
Madam, send you in haste to speake with him,
And I my selfe will stand behind the Arras,
There question you the cause of all his griefe,
And then in loue and nature vnto you, hee'le tell you all:
My Lord, how thinke you on't?

King It likes vs well, Gerterd, what say you?

Queene With all my heart, soone will I send for him.

Cor. My selfe will be that happy messenger,
Who hopes his griefe will be reueal'd to her. *exeunt omnes*
                                        Enter

Enter Hamlet and the Players.

III.ii.

1

Ham. Pronounce me this speech trippingly a the tongue
as I taught thee,
Mary and you mouth it, as a many of your players do
I'de rather heare a towne bull bellow,
Then such a fellow speake my lines.
Nor do not saw the aire thus with your hands,
But giue euery thing his action with temperance.   (fellow,
O it offends mee to the soule, to heare a rebustious periwig
To teare a passion in totters, into very ragges,
To split the eares of the ignoraut, who for the   (noises,
Most parte are capable of nothing but dumbe shewes and
I would haue such a fellow whipt, for o're doing, tarmagant
It out, Herodes Herod.

    players My Lorde, wee haue indifferently reformed that
among vs.
    Ham. The better, the better, mend it all together:
There be fellowes that I haue seene play,
And heard others commend them, and that highly too,
That hauing neither the gate of Christian, Pagan,
Nor Turke, haue so strutted and bellowed,
That you would a thought, some of Natures journeymen
Had made men, and not made them well,
They imitated humanitie, so abhominable:
Take heede, auoyde it.

    players I warrant you my Lord.
    Ham. And doe you heare? let not your Clowne speake
More then is set downe, there be of them I can tell you
That will laugh themselues, to set on some
Quantitie of barren spectators to laugh with them,
Albeit there is some necessary point in the Play
Then to be obserued: O t'is vile, and shewes
A pittifull ambition in the foole that vseth it.
And then you haue some agen, that keepes one sute
Of ieasts, as a man is knowne by one sute of
Apparell, and Gentlemen quotes his ieasts downe

      In

5
6-9
10

12

15
16
40-1

42
32

35

39
16
17
42

45

50

In their tables, before they come to the play, as thus:
Cannot you stay till I eate my porrige? and, you owe me
A quarters wages: and, my coate wants a cullison:
And, your beere is sowre: and, blabbering with his lips,
And thus keeping in his <u>cinkapase</u> of ieasts,
When, God knows, the warme Clowne cannot make a iest
Vnlesse by chance, as the blinde man catcheth a hare:
Maisters tell him of it.

    players We will my Lord.

    Ham. Well, goe make you ready.   *exeunt players.*

    Horatio. Heere my Lord.

    Ham. *Horatio,* thou art euen as iust a man,
As e're my conuersation cop'd withall.

    Hor. O my lord!

    Ham. Nay why should I flatter thee?
Why should the poore be flattered?
What gaine should I receiue by flattering thee,
That nothing hath but thy good minde?
Let flattery sit on those time-pleasing tongs,
To glose with them that loues to heare their praise,
And not with such as thou *Horatio.*
There is a play to night, wherein one Sceane they haue
Comes very neere the murder of my father,
When thou shalt see that Act afoote,
Marke thou the King, doe but obserue his lookes,
For I mine eies will riuet to his face:
And if he doe not bleach, and change at that,
It is a damned ghost that we haue seene.
Horatio, haue a care, obserue him well.

    Hor. My lord, mine eies shall still be on his face,
And not the smallest alteration
That shall appeare in him, but I shall note it.

    Ham. Harke, they come.

    Enter King, Queene, Corambis, and other Lords. (a play?

    King How now son *Hamlet,* how fare you, shall we haue

    Ham. Yfaith the Camelions dish, not capon cramm'd,
                                 feede

Marginal line numbers:
50 *
58
60
61
61 .
64
62
63
65
66-7 *
80
81-2
83
85 .
90
85-6
87
*
93
94
95
97 .
98-110

feede a the ayre.

I father : My lord, you playd in the Vniuerſitie.

   Cor. That I did my L: and I was counted a good actor.

   Ham. What did you enact there?

   Cor. My lord, I did act *Iulius Cæſar*, I was killed
in the Capitoll, *Brutus* killed me.

   Ham. It was a brute parte of him,
To kill ſo capitall a calfe.

Come, be theſe Players ready?

   Queene Hamlet come ſit downe by me.

   Ham. No by my faith mother, heere's a mettle more at-
Lady will you giue me leaue, and ſo forth: (tractiue:
To lay my head in your lappe?

   Ofel. No my Lord.   (trary matters?

   Ham. Vpon your lap, what do you thinke I meant con-

   *Enter in a Dumbe Shew, the King and the Queene, he ſits
    downe in an Arbor, ſhe leaues him : Then enters Luci-
    anus with poyſon in a Viall, and powres it in his eares, and
    goes away : Then the Queene commeth and findes him
    dead : and goes away with the other.*

   Ofel. What meanes this my Lord?   *Enter the Prologue.*

   Ham. This is myching Mallico, that meanes my chiefe.

   Ofel. What doth this meane my lord?

   Ham. you ſhall heare anone, this fellow will tell you all.

   Ofel. Will he tell vs what this ſhew meanes?

   Ham. I, or any ſhew you'le ſhew him,
Be not afeard to ſhew, hee'le not be afeard to tell:
O theſe Players cannot keepe counſell, thei'le tell all.

   Prol. For vs, and for our Tragedie,
Heere ſtowping to your clemencie,
We begge your hearing patiently.

   Ham. I'ſt a prologue, or a poeſie for a ring?

   Ofel. T'is ſhort my Lord.

   Ham. As womens loue.

        Enter the Duke and Dutcheſſe.

   Duke Full fortie yeares are paſt, their date is gone,

        F 3   Since

111
* 115
116-7
119
121
120
• 119-23

*

146
147-8
146
151-2
• 153
155-6
152
159

*

165

Duke & Dutcheſs ſh. be as below (handwritten margin note)

Since happy time ioyn'd both our hearts as one:
And now the blood that fill'd my youthfull veines,
Runnes weakely in their pipes, and all the straines
Of musicke, which whilome pleasde mine eare,
Is now a burthen that Age cannot beare:
And therefore sweete Nature must pay his due,
To heauen must I, and leaue the earth with you.

   Dutchesse O say not so, lest that you kill my heart,
When death takes you, let life from me depart.

   Duke Content thy selfe, when ended is my date,
Thon maist (perchance) haue a more noble mate,
More wise, more youthfull, and one.

   Dutchesse O speake no more, for then I am accurst,
None weds the second, but she kils the first:
A second time I kill my Lord that's dead,
When second husband kisses me in bed.

   Ham. O wormewood, wormewood!

   Duke I doe beleeue you sweete, what now you speake,
But what we doe determine oft we breake,
For our demises stil are ouerthrowne,
Our thoughts are ours, their end's none of our owne:
So thinke you will no second husband wed,
But die thy thoughts, when thy first Lord is dead.

   Dutchesse Both here and there pursue me lasting strife,
If once a widdow, euer I be wife.

   Ham. If she should breake now.

   Duke T'is deeply sworne, sweete leaue me here a while,
My spirites growe dull, and faine I would beguile the tedi-
ous time with sleepe.

   Dutchesse Sleepe rocke thy braine,
And neuer come mischance betweene vs twaine. *exit Lady*

   Ham. Madam, how do you like this play?

   Queene The Lady protests too much.

   Ham. O but shee'le keepe her word.

   King Haue you heard the argument, is there no offence
in it?

                                     Ham.

183-5

186-7

187-9
190
194
195
191
196
197
222

225
232

235

240

Ham. No offence in the world, poyson in iest, poyson in

King What do you call the name of the play? (iest.

Ham. Mouse-trap: mary how trapically: this play is

The image of a murder done in *guyana, Albertus*

Was the Dukes name, his wife *Baptista,*

Father, it is a knauish peece a worke: but what

A that, it toucheth not vs, you and I that haue free

Soules, let the galld iade wince, this is one

Lucianus nephew to the King, Duke.

Ofel. Ya're as good as a *Chorus* my lord.

Ham. I could interpret the loue you beare, if I sawe the

poopies dallying.

Ofel. Y'are very pleasant my lord.

Ham. Who I, your onlie iig-maker, why what shoulde

a man do but be merry? for looke how cheerefully my mo-

ther lookes, my father died within these two houres.

Ofel. Nay, t'is twice two months, my Lord.

Ham. Two months, nay then let the diuell weare blacke,

For i'le haue a sute of Sables: Iesus, two months dead,

And not forgotten yet? nay then there's some

Likelyhood, a gentlemans death may outliue memorie,

But by my faith hee must build churches then,

Or els hee must follow the olde Epitithe,

With hoh, with ho, the hobi-horse is forgot.

Ofel. Your iests are keene my Lord.

Ham. It would cost you a groning to take them off.

Ofel. Still better and worse.

Ham. So you must take your husband, begin. Murdred

Begin, a poxe, leaue thy damnable faces and begin,

Come, the croking rauen doth bellow for reuenge.

Murd. Thoughts blacke, hands apt, drugs fit, and time

Confederate season, else no creature seeing: (agreeing.

Thou mixture rancke, of midnight weedes collected,

With *Hecates* bane thrise blasted, thrise infected,

Thy naturall magicke, and dire propertie,

One wholesome life vsurps immediately. *exit.*

Ham.

The Tragedy of Hamlet.

Ham. He poysons him for his estate.

King Lights, I will to bed.

Cor. The king rises, lights hoe.

Exeunt King and Lordes.

Ham. What, frighted with false fires?

Then let the stricken deere goe weepe,

The Hart vngalled play,

For some must laugh, while some must weepe,

Thus runnes the world away.

Hor. The king is mooued my lord.

Hor. I *Horatio,* i'le take the Ghosts word

For more then all the coyne in *Denmarke.*

—

Enter Roßencraft and Gilderstone.

Roß. Now my lord, how i'st with you?

Ham. And if the king like not the tragedy,

Why then belike he likes it not perdy.

Roß. We are very glad to see your grace so pleasant,

My good lord, let vs againe intreate   (ture

To know of you the ground and cause of your distempera-

Gil. My lord, your mother craues to speake with you.

Ham. We shall obey, were she ten times our mother.

Roß. But my good Lord, shall I intreate thus much?

Ham. I pray will you play vpon this pipe?

Roß. Alas my lord I cannot.

Ham. Pray will you.

Gil. I haue no skill my Lord.

Ham. why looke, it is a thing of nothing,

T'is but stopping of these holes,

And with a little breath from your lips,

It will giue most delicate musick.

Gil. But this cannot wee do my Lord.

Ham. Pray now, pray hartily, I beseech you.

Ros. My lord wee cannot.   (me?

Ham. Why how vnworthy a thing would you make of

You

You would seeme to know my stops, you would play vpon

You would search the very inward part of my hart,   mee,   382

And diue into the secrect of my soule.

Zownds do you thinke Iam easier to be pla'yd   386

On, then a pipe? call mee what Instrument

You will, though you can frett mee, yet you can not   389

Play vpon mee, besides, to be demanded by a spunge.   IV.ii.

    Ros. How a spunge my Lord?   15

    Ham. I sir, a spunge, that sokes vp the kings

Countenance, fauours, and rewardes, that makes   * 17

His liberalitie your store house : but such as you,

Do the king, in the end, best seruise;   18

For hee doth keep you as an Ape doth nuttes,

In the corner of his Iaw, first mouthes you,

Then swallowes you : so when hee hath need

Of you, t'is but squeefing of you,

And spunge, you shall be dry againe, you shall.   23

    Ros. Wel my Lord wee'le take our leaue.

    Ham Farewell, farewell, God blesse you.

       Exit Rossencraft and Gilderstone.   *

        Enter Corambis   III.ii.

    Cor. My lord, the Queene would speake with you.   391

    Ham. Do you see yonder clowd in the shape of a camell?

    Cor. T'is like a camell in deed.   395

    Ham. Now me thinkes it's like a weasel.

    Cor. T'is back't like a weasell.

    Ham. Or like a whale.

    Cor. Very like a whale.   *exit Coram.*

    Ham. Why then tell my mother i'le come by and by.

Good night Horatio.   400

    Hor. Good night vnto your Lordship.   *exit Horatio.*   * 405

    Ham. My mother she hath sent to speake with me:

O God, let ne're the heart of *Nero* enter   410

This soft bosome.

Let me be cruell, not vnnaturall.

        G   I

III.ii.

4.14   I will speake daggers, those sharpe wordes being spent,

4.17   To doe her wrong my soule shall ne're consent.   *exit.*

III.iii.   *Enter the King.*

      King O that this wet that falles vpon my face

46   · Would wash the crime cleere from my conscience!

50   When I looke vp to heauen, I see my trespasse,

37   The earth doth still crie out vpon my fact,

      Pay me the murder of a brother and a king,

      And the adulterous fault I haue committed:

51-2 * O these are sinnes that are vnpardonable:

43-4 Why say thy sinnes were blacker then is ieat,

45-6 Yet may contrition make them as white as snowe:

53-4 I but still to perseuer in a sinne,

      It is an act gainst the vniuersall power,

70 · Most wretched man, stoope, bend thee to thy prayer,

      Aske grace of heauen to keepe thee from despaire.

         hee kneeles.   *enters Hamlet*

73-4   *Ham.* I so, come forth and worke thy last,

75   And thus hee dies: and so am I reuenged:

80 * No, not so: he tooke my father sleeping, his sins brim full,

      And how his soule stoode to the state of heauen

82   Who knowes, saue the immortall powres,

85   And shall I kill him now,

79 · When he is purging of his soule?

79-88 Making his way for heauen, this is a benefit,

89-91 And not reuenge: no, get thee vp agen,   (drunke,

90   When hee's at game swaring, taking his carowse, drinking

91   Or in the incestuous pleasure of his bed,

*   Or at some act that hath no relish

      Of saluation in't, then trip him

95   That his heeles may kicke at heauen,

      And fall as lowe as hel: my mother stayes,

97   This phisicke but prolongs thy weary dayes.   *exit Ham.*

      King My wordes fly vp, my sinnes remaine below.

                           No

No King on earth is safe, if Gods his foe.   *exit King.*
                 Enter Queene and Corambis.
   Cor. Madame, I heare yong Hamlet comming,
I'le shrowde my selfe behinde the Arras.   *exit Cor.*
   Queene Do so my Lord.
   Ham. Mother, mother, O are you here?
How i'st with you mother?
   Queene How i'st with you?
   Ham, I'le tell you, but first weele make all safe.
   Queene Hamlet, thou hast thy father much offended.
   Ham. Mother, you haue my father much offended.
   Queene How now boy?
   Ham. How now mother! come here, sit downe, for you
shall heare me speake.
   Queene What wilt thou doe? thou wilt not murder me:
Helpe hoe.
   Cor. Helpe for the Queene.
   Ham. I a Rat, dead for a Duckat.
Rash intruding foole, farewell,
I tooke thee for thy better.
   Queene Hamlet, what hast thou done?
   Ham. Not so much harme, good mother,
As to kill a king, and marry with his brother.
   Queene How! kill a king!
   Ham. I a King: nay sit you downe, and ere you part,
If you be made of penitrable stuffe,
I'le make your eyes looke downe into your heart,
And see how horride there and blacke it shews.   (words?
   Queene Hamlet, what mean'st thou by these killing
   Ham. Why this I meane, see here, behold this picture,
It is the portraiture, of your deceased husband,
See here a face, to outface *Mars* himselfe,
An eye, at which his foes did tremble at,
A front wherin all vertue are set downe
For to adorne a king, and guild his crowne,
Whose heart went hand in hand euen with that vow,
                         G 2   He

He made to you in marriage, and he is dead:
Murdred, damnably murdred, this was your husband,
Looke you now, here is your husband,
With a face like *Vulcan*.
A looke fit for a murder and a rape,
A dull dead hanging looke, and a hell-bred eie,
To affright children and amaze the world:
And this same haue you left to change with this.
What Diuell thus hath cosoned you at hob-man blinde?
A! haue you eyes and can you looke on him
That slew my father, and your deere husband,
To liue in the incestuous pleasure of his bed?
   Queene O Hamlet, speake no more.
   Ham. To leaue him that bare a Monarkes minde,
For a king of clowts, of very shreads.
   Queene Sweete Hamlet cease.
   Ham. Nay but still to persist and dwell in sinne,
To sweate vnder the yoke of infamie,
To make increase of shame, to seale damnation.
   Queene Hamlet, no more.
   Ham. Why appetite with you is in the waine,
Your blood runnes backeward now from whence it came,
Who'le chide hote blood within a Virgins heart,
When lust shall dwell within a matrons breast?
   Queene Hamlet, thou cleaues my heart in twaine.
   Ham. O throw away the worser part of it, and keepe the
better.

        Enter the ghost in his night gowne.

Saue me, saue me, you gratious
Powers aboue, and houer ouer mee,
With your celestiall wings.
Doe you not come your tardy sonne to chide,
That I thus long haue let reuenge slippe by?
O do not glare with lookes so pittifull!
Lest that my heart of stone yeelde to compassion,

                And

And euery part that should assist reuenge,
Forgoe their proper powers, and fall to pitty.

   Ghost Hamlet, I once againe appeare to thee,   110
To put thee in remembrance of my death: 111
Doe not neglect, nor long time put it off.
But I perceiue by thy distracted lookes,   *her*
Thy mother's fearefull, and she stands amazde: 112
Speake to her Hamlet, for her sex is weake,   115-4
Comfort thy mother, Hamlet, thinke on me.   113
   Ham. How i'st with you Lady?   * 115
   Queene Nay, how i'st with you
That thus you bend your eyes on vacancie,
And holde discourse with nothing but with ayre?   118
   Ham. Why doe you nothing heare?   133
   Queene Not I.   · 133
   Ham. Nor doe you nothing see?   131
   Queene. No neither.   (habite   132
   Ham. No, why see the king my father, my father, in the   134
As he liued, looke you how pale he lookes,   135
See how he steales away out of the Portall,   * 134-6
Looke, there he goes.   *exit ghost.*   136
   Queene Alas, it is the weakenesse of thy braine,   137
Which makes thy tongue to blazon thy hearts griefe:
But as I haue a soule, I sweare by heauen,
I neuer knew of this most horride murder:
But Hamlet, this is onely fantasie,   138
And for my loue forget these idle fits.
   Ham. Idle, no mother, my pulse doth beate like yours,   140
It is not madnesse that possesseth Hamlet.   141
O mother, if euer you did my deare father loue,   *
Forbeare the adulterous bed to night,   159-65
And win your selfe by little as you may,   166-7
In time it may be you wil lothe him quite:
And mother, but assist mee in reuenge,
And in his death your infamy shall die.   · 197
   Queene Hamlet, I vow by that maiesty,

That knowes our thoughts, and lookes into our hearts,
I will conceale, confent, and doe my beſt,
What ſtratagem ſoe're thou ſhalt deuiſe.

   Ham. It is enough, mother good night:
Come ſir, I'le prouide for you a graue,
Who was in life a fooliſh prating knaue.

         Exit Hamlet with the dead body.

        Enter the King and Lordes.

   King Now Gertred, what ſayes our ſonne, how doe you
finde him?

   Queene Alas my lord, as raging as tho ſea:
Whenas he came, I firſt beſpake him faire,
But then he throwes and toſſes me about,
As one forgetting that I was his mother:
At laſt I call'd for help : and as I cried, *Corambis*
Call'd, which Hamlet no ſooner heard, but whips me
Out his rapier, and cries, a Rat, a Rat, and in his rage
The good olde man he killes.

   King Why this his madneſſe will vndoe our ſtate.
Lordes goe to him, inquire the body out.

   Gil. We will my Lord.   *Exeunt Lordes.*

   King Gertred, your ſonne ſhall preſently to England,
His ſhipping is already furniſhed,
And we haue ſent by *Roſſencraſt* and *GilderſIone,*
Our letters to our deare brother of England,
For Hamlets welfare and his happineſſe:
Happly the aire and climate of the Country
May pleaſe him better than his natiue home:
See where he comes.

       Enter Hamlet and the Lordes.

   Gil. My lord, we can by no meanes
Know of him where the body is.

   King Now ſonne Hamlet, where is this dead body?

   Ham. At ſupper, not where he is eating, but

                                Where

III.iv.

198-9

213
216-2
215

IV.i.
6
7

10
10-1
12-1
14
36

IV.iii.
13
12
17
18-20

Where he is eaten, a certaine company of politicke wormes
are euen now at him.

Father, your fatte King, and your leane Beggar
Are but variable seruices, two dishes to one messe:
Looke you, a man may fish with that worme
That hath eaten of a King,
And a Beggar eate that fish,
Which that worme hath caught.

    King What of this?

    Ham. Nothing father, but to tell you, how a King
May go a progresse through the guttes of a Beggar.

    King But sonne *Hamlet*, where is this body?

    Ham. In heau'n, if you chance to misse him there,
Father, you had best looke in the other partes below
For him, aud if you cannot finde him there,
You may chance to nose him as you go vp the lobby.

    King Make haste and finde him out.

    Ham. Nay doe you heare? do not make too much haste,
I'le warrant you hee'le stay till you come.

    King Well sonne *Hamlet*, we in care of you: but specially
in tender preseruation of your health,
The which we price euen as our proper selfe,
It is our minde you forthwith goe for *England*,
The winde sits faire, you shall aboorde to night,
Lord *Rossencraft* and *Gilderstone* shall goe along with you.

    Ham. O with all my heart: farewel mother.

    King Your louing father, *Hamlet*.

    Ham. My mother I say: you married my mother,
My mother is your wife, man and wife is one flesh,
And so (my mother) farewel: for England hoe.

          exeunt all but the king.

    king Gertred, leaue me,
And take your leaue of *Hamlet*,
To England is he gone, ne're to returne:
Our Letters are vnto the King of England,
That on the sight of them, on his allegeance,

                           He

He presently without demaunding why,
That *Hamlet* loose his head, for he must die,
There's more in him than shallow eyes can see:
He once being dead, why then our state is free. *exit.*

Enter Fortenbrasse, Drumme and Souldiers.

Fort. Captaine, from vs goe greete
The king of Denmarke:
Tell him that *Fortenbrasse* nephew to old *Norway,*
Craues a free passe and conduct ouer his land,
According to the Articles agreed on:
You know our Randevous, goe march away. *exeunt all.*

enter King and Queene.

King *Hamlet* is ship't for England, fare him well,
I hope to heare good newes from thence ere long,
If euery thing fall out to our content,
As I doe make no doubt but so it shall.
Queene God grant it may, heau'ns keep my *Hamlet* safe:
But this mischance of olde *Corambis* death,
Hath piersed so the yong *Ofeliaes* heart,
That she, poore maide, is quite bereft her wittes.
King Alas deere heart! And on the other side,
We vnderstand her brother's come from *France,*
And he hath halfe the heart of all our Land,
And hardly hee'le forget his fathers death,
Vnlesse by some meanes he be pacified.
Qu. O see where the yong *Ofelia* is!

Enter Ofelia playing on a Lute, and her hayre
downe singing.

Ofelia How should I your true loue know
From another man?
By his cockle hatte, and his staffe,

And

And his fandall fhoone.　　　　　26

White his fhrowde as mountaine fnowe,　　35

Larded with fweete flowers,　　　37

That bewept to the graue did not goe

With true louers fhowers:　　　・39

He is dead and gone Lady, he is dead and gone,　29-30

At his head a graffe greene turffe,

At his heeles a ftone.　　　32

　　king How i'ft with you fweete *Ofelia*?　40

　　Ofelia Well God yeeld you,　　＊41

It grieues me to fee how they laid him in the cold ground,　70

I could not chufe but weepe:　　69

And will he not come againe?　　190

And will he not come againe?

No, no, hee's gone, and we caft away mone,　・192-8

And he neuer will come againe.　194

His beard as white as fnowe:

All flaxen was his pole,　　196

He is dead, he is gone,　　192-7

And we caft away moane:　　＊

God a mercy on his foule.

And of all chriften foules I pray God.　200

God be with you Ladies, God be with you. *exit Ofelia.*　73-200

　　king A pretty wretch! this is a change indeede:

O Time, how fwiftly runnes our ioyes away?

Content on earth was neuer certaine bred,

To day we laugh and liue, to morrow dead.

How now, what noyfe is that?　　96

　　　　A noyfe within.　　*enter Leartes.*

　　Lear. Stay there vntill I come,　　＊112

O thou vilde king, giue me my father:　115-6

Speake, fay, where's my father?　128

　　king Dead.　　128

　　Lear. Who hath murdred him? fpeake, i'le not　130

Be iuggled with, for he is murdred.　・130

　　Queene True, but not by him.　128

　　　　　　H　　　　　*Leartes*

Lear. By whome, by heau'n I'le be refolued.

122 *king* Let him goe *Gertred*, away, I feare him not,
There's fuch diuinitie doth wall a king,
124 That treafon dares not looke on.
126-8 . Let him goe *Gertred*, that your father is murdred,
150 T'is true, and we moft fory for it,
Being the chiefeft piller of our ftate:
Therefore will you like a moft defperate gamfter,
142 Swoop-ftake-like, draw at friend, and foe, and all?
145 * *Lear.* To his good friends thus wide I'le ope mine arms,
And locke them in my hart, but to his foes,
I will no reconcilement but by bloud.

147-8 *king* Why now you fpeake like a moft louing fonne:
150 And that in foule we forrow for for his death,
151 Your felfe ere long fhall be a witneffe,
Meane while be patient, and content your felfe.

Enter Ofelia as before.

158 *Lear.* Who's this, *Ofelia*? O my deere fifter!
I'ft poffible a yong maides life,
160 * Should be as mortall as an olde mans fawe?
O heau'ns themfelues! how now *Ofelia*?

Ofel. Wel God a mercy, I a bin gathering of floures:
181 Here, here is rew for you,
182 You may call it hearb a grace a Sundayes,
181-3 . Heere's fome for me too : you muft weare your rew
183-4 With a difference, there's a dazie.
175 Here Loue, there's rofemary for you
For remembrance : I pray Loue remember,
And there's panfey for thoughts.

179 * *Lear.* A document in madnes, thoughts, remembrance:
201 O God, O God!
180-4 *Ofelia* There is fennell for you, I would a giu'n you
185 Some violets, but they all withered, when
41 My father died : alas, they fay the owle was
A Bakers daughter, we fee what we are,
43 But can not tell what we fhall be.

For

For bonny sweete Robin is all my ioy.

    Lear. Thoughts & afflictions, torments worse than hell.

    Ofel. Nay Loue, I pray you make no words of this now:

I pray now, you shall sing a downe,

And you a downe a, t'is a the Kings daughter

And the false steward, and if any body

Aske you of any thing, say you this.

To morrow is saint Valentines day,

All in the morning betime,

And a maide at your window,

To be your Valentine:

The yong man rose, and dan'd his clothes,

And dupt the chamber doore,

Let in the maide, that out a maide

Neuer departed more.

Nay I pray marke now,

By gisse, and by saint Charitie,

Away, and fie for shame:

Yong men will doo't when they come too't

By cocke they are too blame.

Quoth she, before you tumbled me,

You promised me to wed.

So would I a done, by yonder Sunne,

If thou hadst not come to my bed.

So God be with you all, God bwy Ladies.

God bwy you Loue.   *exit Ofelia.*

    Lear. Griefe vpon griefe, my father murdered,

My sister thus distracted:

Cursed be his soule that wrought this wicked act.

    king Content you good Leartes for a time,

Although I know your griefe is as a floud,

Brimme full of sorrow, but forbeare a while,

And thinke already the reuenge is done

On him that makes you such a haplesse sonne.

    Lear. You haue preuail'd my Lord, a while I'le striue,

To bury griefe within a tombe of wrath,

        H 2   Which

IV

170
• 171-3
172
47

* 50

• 55
28
59

*

66
• 41-73

* 210
202

Which once vnhearfed, then the world fhall heare
Leartes had a father he held deere.

   king No more of that, ere many dayes be done,
You fhall heare that you do not dreame vpon.   *exeunt om.*

Enter Horatio and the Queene.

   Hor. Madame, your fonne is fafe arriv'de in *Denmarke*,
This letter I euen now receiv'd of him,
Whereas he writes how he efcap't the danger,
And fubtle treafon that the king had plotted,
Being croffed by the contention of the windes,
He found the Packet fent to the king of *England*,
Wherein he faw himfelfe betray'd to death,
As at his next conuerfion with your grace,
He will relate the circumftance at full.

   Queene Then I perceiue there's treafon in his lookes
That feem'd to fugar o're his villanie:
But I will foothe and pleafe him for a time,
For murderous mindes are alwayes jealous,
But know not you *Horatio* where he is?

   Hor. Yes Madame,and he hath appoynted me
To meete him on the eaft fide of the Cittie
To morrow morning.

   Queene O faile not, good *Horatio*, and withall, com-
A mothers care to him, bid him a while   (mend me
Be wary of his prefence, left that he
Faile in that he goes about.

   Hor. Madam, neuer make doubt of that:
I thinke by this the news be come to court:
He is arriv'de, obferue the king, and you fhall
Quickely finde, *Hamlet* being here,
Things fell not to his minde.

   Queene But what became of *Gilderftone* and *Roffencraft*?

   Hor. He being fet afhore, they went for *England*,
And in the Packet there writ down that doome
To be perform'd on them poynted for him:
And by great chance he had his fathers Seale,

So all was done without difcouerie.

   Queene Thankes be to heauen for bleffing of the prince,
Horatio once againe I take my leaue,
With thowfand mothers bleffings to my fonne.

   Horat. Madam adue.

          Enter King and Leartes.

   King. Hamlet from *England!* is it poffible?
What chance is this? they are gone, and he come home.

   Lear. O he is welcome, by my foule he is:
At it my iocund heart doth leape for ioy,
That I fhall liue to tell him, thus he dies.

   king Leartes, content your felfe, be rulde by me,
And you fhall haue no let for your reuenge.

   Lear. My will, not all the world.

   King Nay but Leartes, marke the plot I haue layde,
I haue heard him often with a greedy wifh,
Vpon fome praife that he hath heard of you
Touching your weapon, which with all his heart,
He might be once tasked for to try your cunning.

   Lea. And how for this?

   King Mary Leartes thus: I'le lay a wager,
Shalbe on *Hamlets* fide, and you fhall giue the oddes,
The which will draw him with a more defire,
To try the maiftry, that in twelue venies
You gaine not three of him : now this being granted,
When you are hot in midft of all your play,
Among the foyles fhall a keene rapier lie,
Steeped in a mixture of deadly poyfon,
That if it drawes but the leaft dramme of blood,
In any part of him, he cannot liue:
This being done will free you from fufpition,
And not the deereft friend that *Hamlet* lov'de
Will euer haue Leartes in fufpect.

* 107
156

158
139
141-8
147-8
* 149
67
68

   Lear. My lord, I like it well:
But fay lord *Hamlet* fhould refufe this match.

   King I'le warrant you, wee'le put on you

        H 3   Such

Such a report of singularitie,
Will bring him on, although against his will.
And lest that all should misse,
I'le haue a potion that shall ready stand,
In all his heate when that he calles for drinke,
Shall be his period and our happinesse.

    Lear. T is excellent, O would the time were come!
Here comes the Queene.   *enter the Queene.*

    king How now Gertred, why looke you heauily?

    Queene O my Lord, the yong *Ofelia*
Hauing made a garland of sundry sortes of floures,
Sitting vpon a willow by a brooke,
The enuious sprig broke, into the brooke she fell,
And for a while her clothes spread wide abroade,
Bore the yong Lady vp: and there she sate smiling,
Euen Mermaide-like, twixt heauen and earth,
Chaunting olde sundry tunes vncapable
As it were of her distresse, but long it could not be,
Till that her clothes, being heauy with their drinke,
Dragg'd the sweete wretch to death.

    Lear. So, she is drownde:
Too much of water hast thou *Ofelia*,
Therefore I will not drowne thee in my teares,
Reuenge it is must yeeld this heart releefe,
For woe begets woe, and griefe hangs on griefe.   *exeunt.*
    enter Clowne and an other.

    Clowne I say no, she ought not to be buried
In christian buriall.

    2. Why sir?

    Clowne Mary because shee's drownd.

    2. But she did not drowne her selfe.

    Clowne No, that's certaine, the water drown'd her.

    2. Yea but it was against her will.

    Clowne No, I deny that, for looke you sir, I stand here,
If the water come to me, I drowne not my selfe:
But if I goe to the water, and am there drown'd,

    Ergo

Ergo I am guiltie of my owne death:
Y'are gone, goe y'are gone sir.

   2. I but see, she hath christian buriall,
Because she is a great woman.

   Clowne Mary more's the pitty, that great folke
Should haue more authoritie to hang or drowne
Themselues, more than other people:
Goe fetch me a stope of drinke, but before thou
Goest, tell me one thing, who buildes strongest,
Of a Mason, a Shipwright, or a Carpenter?

   2. Why a Mason, for he buildes all of stone,
And will indure long.

   Clowne That's prety, too't agen, too't agen.

   2. Why then a Carpenter, for he buildes the gallowes,
And that brings many a one to his long home.

   Clowne Prety agen, the gallowes doth well, mary howe
dooes it well ? the gallowes dooes well to them that doe ill,
goe get thee gone:
And if any one aske thee hereafter, say,
A Graue-maker, for the houses he buildes
Last till Doomes-day. Fetch me a stope of beere, goe.

       Enter Hamlet and Horatio.
   Clowne A picke-axe and a spade,
A spade for and a winding sheete,
Most fit it is, for t'will be made,   *he throwes vp a shouel.*
For such a ghest most meete.

   Ham. Hath this fellow any feeling of himselfe,
That is thus merry in making of a graue?
See how the slaue joles their heads against the earth.

   Hor. My lord, Custome hath made it in him seeme no-
   Clowne A pick-axe and a spade, a spade,   (thing.
For and a winding sheete,
Most fit it is for to be made,
For such a ghest most meet.

   Ham. Looke you, there's another *Horatio.*

                        Why

21-2
28
27
•30
32
67-8
46
*47-8

51-6
49
•50
51-2
52-3
67
65
*66
67-8

102

•

105
73
74
84
*75-6
102

105

•

V.i.
106-7
111
111
110
107-8 ·
114
120
119

*
123

126
92 ·

94
126

128 *
145

141

·
144
146
148-50
150-2
152-3 *
153
178-9

181
183-4 ·
184

Why mai't not be the scull of some Lawyer?
Me thinkes he should indite that fellow
Of an action of Batterie, for knocking
Him about the pate with's shouel: now where is your
Quirkes and quillets now, your vouchers and
Double vouchers, your leases and free-holde,
And tenements? why that same boxe there will scarse
Holde the conueiance of his land, and must
The honor lie there? O pittifull transformance!
I prethee tell me *Horatio*,
Is parchment made of sheep-skinnes?

   Hor. I my Lorde, and of calues-skinnes too.

   Ham. Ifaith they prooue themselues sheepe and calues
That deale with them, or put their trust in them.
There's another, why may not that be such a ones
Scull, that praised my Lord such a ones horse,
When he meant to beg him? *Horatio*, I prethee
Lets question yonder fellow.
Now my friend, whose graue is this?

   Clowne Mine sir.

   Ham. But who must lie in it?   (sir.

   Clowne If I should say, I should, I should lie in my throat

   Ham. What man must be buried here?

   Clowne No man sir,

   Ham. What woman?

   Clowne. No woman neither sir, but indeede
One that was a woman.

   Ham. An excellent fellow by the Lord *Horatio*,
This seauen yeares haue I noted it: the toe of the pesant,
Comes so neere the heele of the courtier,
That hee gawles his kibe, I prethee tell mee one thing,
How long will a man lie in the ground before hee rots?

   Clowne Ifaith sir, if hee be not rotten before
He be laide in, as we haue many pocky corses,
He will last you, eight yeares, a tanner
Will last you eight yeares full out, or nine.

                                 Ham.

Ham. And why a tanner?

Clowne Why his hide is so tanned with his trade,
That it will holde out water, that's a parlous
Deuourer of your dead body, a great soaker.
Looke you, heres a scull hath bin here this dozen yeare,
Let me see, I euer since our last king *Hamlet*
Slew *Fortenbrasse* in combat, yong *Hamlets* father,
Hee that's mad.

   Ham. I mary, how came he madde?

Clowne Ifaith very strangely, by loosing of his wittes.

Ham. Vpon what ground?

Clowne A this ground, in *Denmarke.*

Ham. Where is he now?

Clowne Why now they sent him to *England.*

Ham. To *England!* wherefore?

Clowne Why they say he shall haue his wittes there,
Or if he haue not, t'is no great matter there,
It will not be seene there.

Ham. Why not there?

Clowne Why there they say the men are as mad as he.

Ham. Whose scull was this?

Clowne This, a plague on him, a madde rogues it was,
He powred once a whole flagon of Rhenish of my head,
Why do not you know him? this was one *Yorickes* scull.

   Ham. Was this? I prethee let me see it, alas poore *Yoricke*
I knew him *Horatio,*
A fellow of infinite mirth, he hath caried mee twenty times
vpon his backe, here hung those lippes that I haue Kissed a
hundred times, and to see, now they abhorre me : Wheres
your iests now *Yoricke?* your flashes of meriment : now go
to my Ladies chamber, and bid her paint her selfe an inch
thicke, to this she must come *Yoricke. Horatio,* I prethee
tell me one thing, doost thou thinke that *Alexander* looked
thus?

   Hor. Euen so my Lord.

   Ham. And smelt thus?

                        I   *Hor.*

185
• 190
156
157-61
161
171
* 172-4
176
161-2
• 163
166
166-7
169
168
* 170
192
196
197
194-8
• 200-3
203
204-5
207
206
* 208-10
213
214
215-8
•
221

Hor. I my lord, no otherwise.

Ham. No, why might not imagination worke, as thus of *Alexander*, *Alexander* died, *Alexander* was buried, *Alexander* became earth, of earth we make clay, and *Alexander* being but clay, why might not time bring to passe, that he might stoppe the boung hole of a beere barrell? Imperious *Cæsar* dead and turnd to clay, Might stoppe a hole, to keepe the winde away.

     Enter King and Queene, Leartes, and other lordes,
       with a Priest after the coffin.

Ham. What funerall's this that all the Court laments? It shews to be some noble parentage: Stand by a while.

Lear. What ceremony else? say, what ceremony else?

Priest My Lord, we haue done all that lies in vs, And more than well the church can tolerate, She hath had a Dirge sung for her maiden soule: And but for fauour of the king, and you, She had beene buried in the open fieldes, Where now she is allowed christian buriall.

Lear. So, I tell thee churlish Priest, a ministring Angell shall my sister be, when thou liest howling.

Ham. The faire *Ofelia* dead!

Queene Sweetes to the sweete, farewell: I had thought to adorne thy bridale bed, faire maide, And not to follow thee vnto thy graue.

Lear. Forbeare the earth a while: sister farewell:

     Leartes leapes into the graue.

Now powre your earth on, *Olympus* hie, And make a hill to o're top olde *Pellon*:   *Hamlet leapes* Whats he that coniures so?   *in after Leartes*

Ham. Beholde tis I, *Hamlet* the Dane.

Lear. The diuell take thy soule.

Ham. O thou praiest not well, I prethee take thy hand from off my throate, For there is something in me dangerous,

                         Which

Which let thy wisedome feare, holde off thy hand:
I lou'de *Ofelia* as deere as twenty brothers could:
Shew me what thou wilt doe for her:
Wilt fight, wilt fast, wilt pray,
Wilt drinke vp vessels, eate a crocadile? Ile doo't:
Com'st thou here to whine?
And where thou talk'st of burying thee a liue,
Here let vs stand: and let them throw on vs,
Whole hills of earth, till with the heighth therof,
Make Oosell as a Wart.

    King. Forbeare *Leartes*, now is hee mad, as is the sea,
Anone as milde and gentle as a Doue:
Therfore a while giue his wilde humour scope.

    Ham. What is the reason sir that you wrong mee thus?
I neuer gaue you cause: but stand away,
A Cat will meaw, a Dog will haue a day.

           Exit Hamlet and Horatio.

    Queene. Alas, it is his madnes makes him thus,
And not his heart, *Leartes.*

    King. My lord, t'is so: but wee'le no longer trifle,
This very day shall *Hamlet* drinke his last,
For presently we meane to send to him,
Therfore *Leartes* be in readynes.

    Lear. My lord, till then my soule will not bee quiet.

    King. Come *Gertred*, wee'l haue *Leartes*, and our sonne,
Made friends and Louers, as besittes them both,
Euen as they tender vs, and loue their countrie.

    Queene God grant they may.   *exeunt omnes.*

        Enter Hamlet and Horatio

    Ham. beleeue mee, it greeues mee much *Horatio*,
That to *Leartes* I forgot my selfe:
For by my selfe me thinkes I feele his griefe,
Though there's a difference in each others wrong.

       Enter a Bragart Gentleman.

    Horatio, but marke yon water-flie,
The Court knowes him, but hee knowes not the Court.

          I 2   *Gen.*

V.i.
286
292
294
298
300
302
304
*306
295
309
312
·313
315
307
*308
320
322
321
·319
V.ii.
*75
77-8
·84

V.ii.

Gent. Now God saue thee, sweete prince *Hamlet.*

Ham. And you sir: foh, how the muske-cod smels!

92-3   *Gen.* I come with an embassage from his maiesty to you

94   *Ham.* I shall sir giue you attention:

98 .   By my troth me thinkes t'is very colde.

100   *Gent.* It is indeede very rawish colde.

101-2   *Ham.* T''is hot me thinkes.

103   *Gent.* Very swoltery hote:

154   The King, sweete Prince, hath layd a wager on your side,

*   Six Barbary horse, against six french rapiers,

With all their acoutrements too, a the carriages:

159   In good faith they are very curiously wrought.

161   *Ham.* The cariages sir, I do not know what you meane.

164   *Gent.* The girdles, and hangers sir, and such like.

166 .   *Ham.* The worde had beene more cosin german to the

phrase, if he could haue carried the canon by his side,

171   And howe's the wager? I vnderstand you now.

Gent. Mary sir, that yong Leartes in twelue venies

At Rapier and Dagger do not get three oddes of you,

*   And on your side the King hath laide,

And desires you to be in readinesse.

175   *Ham.* Very well, if the King dare venture his wager,

183   I dare venture my skull: when must this be?

184   *Gent.* My Lord, presently, the king, and her maiesty,

212   With the rest of the best iudgement in the Court,

.   Are comming downe into the outward pallace.

212-3   *Ham.* Goe tell his maiestie, I wil attend him.

186   *Gent.* I shall deliuer your most sweet answer.   *exit.*

187   *Ham.* You may sir, none better, for y'are spiced,

*   Else he had a bad nose could not smell a foole.

Hor. He will disclose himselfe without inquirie.

222   *Ham.* Beleeue me *Horatio*, my hart is on the sodaine

223   Very sore, all here about.

227   *Hor.* My lord forbeare the challenge then.

230 .   *Ham.* No *Horatio*, not I, if danger be now,

232-0   Why then it is not to come, theres a predestinate prouidence

in

in the fall of a sparrow : heere comes the King.

231

Enter King, Queene, Leartes, Lordes.

King Now sonne *Hamlet*, we haue laid vpon your head, 236-71
And make no question but to haue the best.

Ham. Your maiestie hath laide a the weaker side. •272

King We doubt it not, deliuer them the foiles. 273-0

Ham. First *Leartes*, heere's my hand and loue, 237
Protesting that I neuer wrongd *Leartes*. 244

If *Hamlet* in his madnesse did amisse, 246

That was not *Hamlet*, but his madnes did it, * 247-8

And all the wrong I e're did to *Leartes*, 241-3

I here proclaime was madnes, therefore lets be at peace, 243-53

And thinke I haue shot mine arrow o're the house, 254

And hurt my brother. 255

Lear. Sir I am satisfied in nature, •255

But in termes of honor I'le stand aloofe, 257-8

And will no reconcilement,

Till by some elder maisters of our time

I may be satisfied.

King Giue them the foiles. 260

Ham. I'le be your foyle *Leartes*, these foyles, * 270

Haue all a laught, come on sir : *a hit.* 266

Lear. No none. *Heere they play:* 276-91

Ham. Iudgement. 291S.D.

Gent. A hit, a most palpable hit. 291

Lear. Well, come againe. *They play againe.* •292

Ham. Another. Iudgement. 292

Lear. I, I grant, a tuch, a tuch. 296

King Here *Hamlet*, the king doth drinke a health to thee 297

Queene Here *Hamlet*, take my napkin, wipe thy face. 293-4

King Giue him the wine. * 299

Ham. Set it by, I'le haue another bowt first, 294

I'le drinke anone. 295

Queene Here *Hamlet*, thy mother drinkes to thee. 295

Shee drinkes. 300

King Do not drinke *Gertred* : O t'is the poysned cup! 301-3

I 3 *Ham.*

308
309
311
306

308

314
320 *
322
316

318
324-6 .

328-30

327-32
333-6 *
337
338
340
340
343-4 .
352

356 *
360
363
364

Ham. *Leartes* come, you dally with me,
I pray you paſſe with your moſt cunningſt play.
 Lear. I! ſay you ſo? haue at you,
Ile hit you now my Lord:
And yet it goes almoſt againſt my conſcience.
 Ham. Come on ſir.

They catch one anothers Rapiers, and both are wounded,
Leartes falles downe, the Queene falles downe and dies.

 King Looke to the Queene.
 Queene O the drinke, the drinke, *Hamlet*, the drinke.
 Ham. Treaſon, ho, keepe the gates.
 Lords How iſt my Lord *Leartes*?
 Lear. Euen as a coxcombe ſhould,
Fooliſhly ſlaine with my owne weapon:
Hamlet, thou haſt not in thee halfe an houre of life,
The fatall Inſtrument is in thy hand.
Vnbated and inuenomed: thy mother's poyſned
That drinke was made for thee.
 Ham. The poyſned Inſtrument within my hand?
Then venome to thy venome, die damn'd villaine:
Come drinke, here lies thy vnion here. *The king dies.*
 Lear. O he is iuſtly ſerued:
Hamlet, before I die, here take my hand,
And withall, my loue: I doe forgiue thee. *Leartes dies.*
 Ham. And I thee, O I am dead *Horatio*, fare thee well.
 Hor. No, I am more an antike Roman,
Then a Dane, here is ſome poiſon left.
 Ham. Vpon my loue I charge thee let it goe,
O fie *Horatio*, and if thou ſhouldſt die,
What a ſcandale wouldſt thou leaue behinde?
What tongue ſhould tell the ſtory of our deaths,
If not from thee? O my heart ſinckes *Horatio*,
Mine eyes haue loſt their ſight, my tongue his vſe:
Farewel *Horatio*, heauen receiue my ſoule. *Ham. dies.*
            Enter

Enter Voltemar and the Ambaſſadors from England.
enter Fortenbraſſe with his traine.

Fort. Where is this bloudy ſight?

Hor. If aught of woe or wonder you'ld behold,
Then looke vpon this tragicke ſpectacle.

Fort. O imperious death! how many Princes
Haſt thou at one draft bloudily ſhot to death?   *(land,*

Ambaſſ. Our ambaſſie that we haue brought from *Eng-*
Where be theſe Princes that ſhould heare vs ſpeake?
O moſt moſt vnlooked for time! vnhappy country.

Hor. Content your ſelues, Ile ſhew to all, the ground,
The firſt beginning of this Tragedy:
Let there a ſcaffold be rearde vp in the market place,
And let the State of the world be there:
Where you ſhall heare ſuch a ſad ſtory tolde,
That neuer mortall man could more vnfolde.

Fort. I haue ſome rights of memory to this kingdome,
Which now to claime my leiſure doth inuite mee:
Let foure of our chiefeſt Captaines
Beare *Hamlet* like a ſouldier to his graue:
For he was likely, had he liued,
To a prou'd moſt royall.
Take vp the bodie, ſuch a ſight as this
Becomes the fieldes, but here doth much amiſſe.

Finis

373
374

375-7

*

380

390
391
389
396
·391

400
401
406
*

409
412
413